CAMBRIDGE SOUTH ASIAN STUDIES

SOUTH INDIAN FACTORY WORKERS

CAMBRIDGE SOUTH ASIAN STUDIES

These monographs are published by the Syndics of Cambridge University Press in association with the Cambridge University Centre for South Asian Studies. The following books have been published in this series:

1 S. Gopal: *British Policy in India, 1858–1905*
2 J. A. B. Palmer: *The Mutiny Outbreak at Meerut in 1857*
3 A. Das Gupta: *Malabar in Asian Trade, 1740–1800*
4 G. Obeyesekere: *Land Tenure in Village Ceylon*
5 H. L. Erdman: *The Swatantra Party and Indian Conservatism*
6 S. N. Mukherjee: *Sir William Jones: A Study in Eighteenth-Century British Attitudes to India*
7 Abdul Majed Khan: *The Transition in Bengal, 1756–1775: A Study of Saiyid Muhammad Reza Khan*
8 Radhe Shyam Rungta: *The Rise of Business Corporations in India, 1851–1900*
9 Pamela Nightingale: *Trade and Empire in Western India, 1784–1806*
10 Amiya Kumar Bagchi: *Private Investment in India, 1900–1939*
11 Judith M. Brown: *Gandhi's Rise to Power: Indian Politics, 1915–1922*
12 Mary C. Carras: *The Dynamics of Indian Political Factions*
13 P. Hardy: *The Muslims of British India*
14 Gordon Johnson: *Provincial Politics and Indian Nationalism*
15 Marguerite S. Robinson: *Political Structure in a Changing Sinhalese Village*
16 Francis Robinson: *Separation among Indian Muslims: The Politics of the United Provinces' Muslims, 1860–1923*
17 Christopher John Baker: *The Politics of South India, 1920–1936*
18 David Washbrook: *The Emergence of Provincial Politics: The Madras Presidency, 1870–1920*
19 Deepak Nayyar: *India's Exports and Export Policies in the 1960s*
20 Mark Holmström: *South Indian Factory Workers: Their Life and Their World*

SOUTH INDIAN FACTORY WORKERS

Their life and their world

MARK HOLMSTRÖM

Lecturer in Social Anthropology
University of East Anglia

CAMBRIDGE UNIVERSITY PRESS

CAMBRIDGE

LONDON · NEW YORK · MELBOURNE

CAMBRIDGE UNIVERSITY PRESS
Cambridge, New York, Melbourne, Madrid, Cape Town, Singapore, São Paulo

Cambridge University Press
The Edinburgh Building, Cambridge CB2 8RU, UK

Published in the United States of America by Cambridge University Press, New York

www.cambridge.org
Information on this title: www.cambridge.org/9780521211345

First published 1976
This digitally printed version 2008

A catalogue record for this publication is available from the British Library

Library of Congress Cataloguing in Publication data
Holmström, Mark, 1934–
South Indian factory workers.
(Cambridge South Asian studies)
Bibliography: p.
Includes index.
1. Labor and laboring classes–Bangalore, India (City)
2. Industrial sociology–India–Bangalore (City)
I. Title. II. Series.
HD8690.B352H64 1976   301.44′42′095487   75-46205

ISBN 978-0-521-21134-5 hardback
ISBN 978-0-521-04812-5 paperback

TO RADHIKA AND SAVITRI

CONTENTS

List of tables	*page* viii
Acknowledgments	ix
On the spelling of Indian words	xi
1	Introduction: the problems	1
2	Bangalore and its factory workers	8
3	Life as a factory worker	27
4	Some careers	86
5	The structure of a career	122
6	Conclusions	136
	Bibliography	148
	Index	151

TABLES

1 Population of Bangalore Urban Agglomeration, by work, 1971   *page* 13
2 Industrial workers as a percentage of all workers and of
   total population in India's six largest cities, 1961   14
3 Organized sector employment in Bangalore District, by
   industry, 1971   15
4 The four sample factories   19
5 Workers in the four factories, by age (both samples)   20
6 Years of service in present factory (both samples)   21
7 Basic salaries in rupees (both samples)   21
8 General education (both samples)   23
9 Formal technical qualifications (both samples)   24
10 Religion (both samples, and Bangalore in 1961)   25
11 Scheduled Castes (Harijans) (both samples, and Bangalore
   in 1971)   25
12 Language (both samples, and Bangalore)   25
13 State of birth (both samples)   26
14 Where workers spent their early childhood (case study
   sample)   28
15 Caste or sect, caste category or religion (case study sample)   32
16 Father's occupation and caste category or religion (case
   study sample)   35
17 Paternal grandfather's occupation and caste category or
   religion (case study sample)   36
18 Age, general education and formal technical qualifications
   (random sample, men)   39
19 Method of recruitment (case study sample)   43
20 Was a relative already in the factory when this worker
   applied? (random sample)   43
21 Number of previous jobs (both samples, men)   45
22 Age at appointment to present job (both samples, men), and
   mean number of previous jobs (random sample only, men)   45
23 Promotions (grade to grade) and years of service (random
   sample)   54
24 Workers, grades and salaries in one private factory (permanent
   employees only)   59
25 Total work force of the same factory, by conditions of
   employment (permanent, temporary etc.)   60
26 Opinions about caste and intermarriage (case study sample)   83

ACKNOWLEDGMENTS

My first debt is to the people this book is about: factory workers and their families who gave up their spare time to talk to me, entertained me in their homes, and in many cases gave me their warm and generous friendship; also the managements of the four factories, who talked to me frankly and at length, and who allowed me to visit the factories freely and to examine the files which each factory keeps on its work force. As I explained to them at the time, I cannot name these people, for this would make it too easy to identify the factories. Some of them will read this book, and I ask them to accept this general acknowledgment of the help they have given me.

There are others whose assistance I can acknowledge openly: Professor R. P. Misra of the Institute of Development Studies at the University of Mysore, and the authorities of that university, under whose auspices and guidance the study was made; Shri J. P. Naik, Member-Secretary of the Indian Council of Social Science Research; Dr T. N. Madan; Usha Panini, who was doing fieldwork in Bangalore at the same time; Dr K. D. Sridharan, Director of the National Institute of Social Science, Bangalore; Shri M. Jayaram Iyer, Regional Director of Workers' Education; B. V. Raman, D. L. N. Rao and Lukas Vallatharai, who did the statistical work; Professor R. P. Dore and Ursula Sharma, whose detailed criticism of the first draft of this book forced me to change my position in some respects, and in others to defend it; Lynn Hieatt, of Cambridge University Press; and my father, who made the index. I would have achieved very little without the support and advice of my wife, Lakshmi.

I am grateful to the Government of India, who allowed me to make the study; to the Ministry of Overseas Development (then the Overseas Development Administration), who generously paid most of the costs; and to the Overseas Studies Committee at the University of East Anglia, who paid the rest. The views expressed are my own: they do not reflect those of the Ministry or of the Indian Government, who gave me a free hand.

University of East Anglia, Norwich   Mark Holmström
December 1975

ON THE SPELLING OF INDIAN WORDS

Kannad'a and Tamil are the main languages in Bangalore. Important minorities speak Telugu, Urdu, Hindi, and Malayalam.

Indian words are spelt here in a new way. The common transliteration uses diacritical marks (as in dhūṇḍnā), which are hard to print and type, blur the outline of words, and are easily left out: the result is a loss of important information. A simple, practical, but accurate transliteration – like the new Chinese Pinyin – would be useful for many purposes. Though this book does not contain very many Indian words or names, I explain the method in detail here, as I hope it will catch on.

I have tried to express every phoneme by a single letter or a diphthong, as in English. This requires one extra sign, provisionally a raised point (˙): it can be typed as an apostrophe, and any well-designed substitute (like ') would do. It is written as a separate letter, not an accent.

This sign makes the preceding consonant(s) retroflex (mand'al, Krisn'a) or the preceding vowel nasal (mai˙huu˙). It modifies some consonants in other ways (r˙ for Tamil ழ; there is no need to distinguish ன from ங n). Long vowels are doubled (ee, oo are *not* as in English, but stand for long e, o in southern languages: in languages like Hindi e, o are always long). Other digraphs include sh for the palatal sibilant (not the retroflex s˙, usually written sh or ṣ) and zh (Tamil ழ); n can stand for ng, ny, or n according to context. Both c and ch are like English ch (but Tamil c is often like s). Unnecessary letters are left out (peria neerru manram, not periya neerr'u manr'am).

I use the more familiar spelling of a few words, like Brahman, Tamil.

Hindi (Devanagari) alphabet (phonemically like Kannad'a):

> a aa i ii u uu ri e ai a˙ ah
> k kh g gh n(ng-)[1] c ch j jh n(ny) t˙ t˙h d˙ d˙h n˙
> t th d dh n p ph b bh m y r l v sh s˙ s h

> Dotted consonants: q kh˙ g˙ z r˙ r˙h f

Tamil alphabet:

> a aa i ii u uu e ee ai o oo au q
> k/g[2] n(ng-) c/j n(ny) t˙/d˙ n˙ t/d n p/b m y r l v zh l˙ r˙ n

> Grantha letters: j s˙ s h ks˙

---

[1] The longer forms in brackets are used only when the context requires them.
[2] The voiced forms after nasals, or between vowels (where they may become fricatives), or in borrowed words.

I

Introduction: the problems

This book is a report on a short study of workers from four factories in Bangalore – an industrial city of some 1.7 million people – which I made in 1971. The study was designed to answer questions about the situation and thinking of workers in modern, capital-intensive factories, and to show how the methods of social anthropology can be used in the study of urban work, especially of new occupations in India.

It is based on case studies of workers and their families, also on statistical material from the managements' files on workers and from other sources, and interviews with managers and union officials. My justification for treating large-scale problems in a short study is that I spent fifteen months doing fieldwork in Bangalore in 1964–5, mainly among industrial workers, and I know the local background well; and that this is a pilot study in a field where there is plenty of research but not much of this kind. The conclusions need to be tested in more extensive studies of other workers, especially casual labourers and men who work in small workshops.

Problems in the sociology of industrial India

I made this study because of my interest in some questions in the sociology of industrial India, which have practical implications (though it is not my business – as a foreign observer – to suggest policies). Broadly speaking, these questions are about the social consequences of high-technology, capital-intensive industrialization and the conditions for it. There are large-scale consequences (for the country, and for those outside industry) and small-scale consequences (for industrial workers and their relatives). This book is mainly about the latter, but the findings have wider implications as well.

Some common mistakes can be disposed of at the beginning: like the idea of a single main line of development or evolution, from traditional, rural-folk society to a uniform type of modern, urban-industrial society, or the confusion of industrialization with urbanization.[1]

[1] e.g. in L. Wirth, 'Urbanism as a way of life', *American Journal of Sociology*, 44:1 (1938), 1–24 (p. 1); R. Redfield, *The little community, and Peasant society and*

I

Introduction: the problems

Other statements made or implied in writing on the subject cannot be disposed of so easily, but need to be tested; for example:

- that industrial workers in countries like India are not 'committed' to industrial work and/or town life as workers in the older industrial countries are supposed to be: they cannot adapt easily to rational bureaucratic organization, regular time-keeping, and career patterns which successful industrialization demands;[2]
- alternatively, they may well be committed, but this commitment can best be put to productive use in a paternalistic type of organization the worker can identify with, where contractual rights and duties are not as sharply defined as they are supposed to be in the 'West': this kind of lifetime commitment *to a firm* being a convenient bridge between the collectivist traditional society and individualistic modern industrial society;[3]
- that industrial workers are a privileged enclave or élite in a dual economy, sharply cut off by their living conditions, life chances and attitudes from those outside the 'organized sector' (the Indian term for the larger firms covered by factory and social security legislation, with union rights entrenched by law etc.): this could imply either that they are very fortunate but someone has to be for industrialization to occur; or that they are so at others' expense, perhaps because of 'urban bias' in planning, and that the others (the peasantry and the 'unorganized sector') get the 'backwash' of industrialization not the benefits;[4]
- that there are viable (and, by implication, better) *alternatives*

culture (Chicago, 1960); and the 'folk–urban continuum' school. Wirth and Redfield were wrong, but at least they made explicit, and testable, what most people had taken for granted and some still do. I do not think it useful to reopen the argument here. For a stimulating discussion of unilinear and other models of social evolution, see E. Gellner, *Thought and change* (London, 1964).

[2] See J. S. Slotkin, *From field to factory* (New York, 1960); C. A. Myers, *Labor problems in the industrialization of India* (Cambridge, Mass., 1958); W. E. Moore, *Industrialization and labor* (New York, 1965); and W. E. Moore and A. S. Feldman (eds.), *Labor commitment and social change in developing areas* (New York, 1960), esp. 'Commitment of the industrial labor force', by the editors (pp. 1ff.). M. D. Morris criticizes the idea of commitment in 'The labor market in India' in *ibid.* pp. 173–200, and in his *The emergence of an industrial labor force in India* (Berkeley, 1965).

[3] This is roughly R. P. Dore's argument (though he thinks 'paternalism' is the wrong word for modern industrial organization in Japan). See his *City life in Japan* (London, 1958), esp. ch. 24; his *British factory – Japanese factory* (London, 1973); and the discussion here on p. 144.

[4] See M. Lipton, 'Strategy for agriculture: urban bias and rural planning' in P. Streeten and Lipton (eds.), *The crisis of Indian planning* (London, 1968), pp. 83–147; A. G. Frank, 'Sociology of development and underdevelopment of

2

Three questions

to high-technology industrialization, as distinct from *complementary* labour-intensive methods, 'intermediate' or 'appropriate technologies'.

These arguments may conceal ideological assumptions: e.g. that the determining factors which have made western countries rich are rational bureaucratic organization and entrepreneurship; that development depends on changing traditional attitudes and values;[5] that a decentralized, mainly rural society is best; or that a flourishing class of small businessmen makes for political stability and social equality. I shall not go into these assumptions in detail, though all of them seem to me very doubtful.

The kinds of evidence needed to test such statements include large-scale economic surveys, of which there are many in India; questionnaire-based surveys of attitudes and careers; and more detailed, first-hand studies of the life experience and thinking of groups affected by industrialization. This is what I have tried to achieve: to build up as full a picture as possible of people's understanding of their situation, and to match this with any external, statistical and large-scale information that is available – to put together two pictures of their situation and life experience, as they see it, and as I see it (with more outside information, theory, and bases for comparison, but without their experience), relating the two views in a rational and systematic way, but not reducing one to the other deterministically. At the beginning of chapter 4 (which consists of commented case studies of individual workers) I say more about the special problems involved in applying this anthropological method to an industrial society.

Three questions

In this study I concentrated on three kinds of question:

1. *Who are the factory workers?* What is their place in Indian urban and national society; their backgrounds, castes, education, places of

sociology', *Catalyst*, Summer 1967, repr. in Frank, *Latin America: underdevelopment or revolution* (New York, 1969), pp. 21–94.
    This argument is now heard more often than the 'commitment' argument, with the shift in emphasis from problems of recruitment and 'manpower planning' to un- and underemployment: see D. Turnham, *The employment problem in less developed countries* (Paris, 1971); and D. Lal, 'Poverty and unemployment: a question of policy', *South Asian Review*, 5:4 (1972), 305–12.
[5] See G. Myrdal, *Asian drama: an inquiry into the poverty of nations* (London, 1968). D. C. McClelland offers a behaviouristic technology for changing attitudes directly in 'The achievement motive in economic growth' in B. F. Hoselitz and W. E. Moore (eds.), *Industrialization and society* (Paris, 1963), pp. 74–96.

3

origin, recruitment, promotion, prospects, incomes, household composition etc.? Are they (or are they likely to remain) a privileged élite in a dual economy? How steep are the gradations (in economic condition, life chances and attitudes) separating factory workers from other town dwellers, e.g. the mass of people employed in small workshops and services, or as casual labourers, or unemployed? What kinds of relations do they have with other people (kinship obligations, economic relations, common membership in groups, are they supporting the unemployed, and so on)?

2. *Factory workers' understanding of their own situation*, both individually (their prospects, choices open to them, the extent to which they can control their own future) and as a group or class. (Do they see themselves as an aristocracy of labour or a group with common interests? Which kinds of people do they identify with or want to be distinguished from?) Their values and objectives (status or a certain life style, social equality, the fulfilment of family obligations, security *versus* income etc.). How accurate is their assessment of their situation, in the light of external facts like the firms' policies, the labour market and population pressures?

3. More specifically, *the idea of a 'job' and of a 'career'*: the career as part (or the focus) of a man's life, and a stage in the family's development over generations (or in some other long-term historical process). Career histories and intentions, and how realistic these are. Is a factory job regarded as property, like the right to perform a specialized service in the so-called village jajmaani system (as apparently it was at other times and places in industrial India[6])? As the result of unpredictable economic forces entirely beyond one's control? As a stage in a career the individual makes for himself? As a Japanese-style lifetime commitment? There are many other possibilities.

The evidence

My evidence consists, first, of case studies of 104 workers from four factories: two in the public sector, making electrical equipment and machinery, and two private ones, making car components and other engineering products. I have avoided saying exactly what the four factories produce, in order to make them slightly harder to identify: those who know Bangalore can narrow the field. I have taken more stringent precautions to disguise informants. Some case studies are quite detailed and record several conversations with a worker and his

---

[6] See R. D. Lambert, *Workers, factories and social change in India* (Princeton, 1963).

family; many are based on one interview. There were a number of topics to which I tried to direct conversations, and specific pieces of information I wanted from each person, but there was no standard interview schedule: I concentrated on whatever was of most interest to the informant and let the conversation develop. Some factual information was coded afterwards on cards, as were the answers to some questions of opinion, though I am more doubtful about their value for statistical analysis.

These case studies are filled out by observations of events like union meetings, a one-day strike, and weddings; interviews with managements and outside union leaders; and odd conversations with people I met around the factories, in cafés, in areas where factory workers live, and anywhere else. I drew heavily on the background knowledge of Bangalore I had acquired in fifteen months' fieldwork in an urban village, in 1964–5,[7] and in a few months' fieldwork among other groups in Bangalore, just before this study of workers' careers began. I have used the 'ethnographic present' tense: when I write that people 'do' or 'say' something, this means they did or said it in 1971.

The case study sample of 104 workers is not strictly random, because I talked to most workers at their homes, and worked through personal introductions to avoid turning up on the doorstep as a stranger with a list of questions. (Somewhere Srinivas describes the Indian peasant fleeing when he sees the sociologist approaching with a questionnaire rolled up like an umbrella.) But the sample was as random as I could make it: I tried to get a fair spread of skilled and unskilled workers, young and old, different castes and so on. To supplement these personal statements by a small sample of workers, I examined a random sample of the personal files which managements keep on each worker (containing a record of promotions, training, personal history, the original letter of application for the job etc.). I did this mainly to find out how typical the case study sample was of the work force in the four factories, and how typical this work force was of the whole urban population (using material from the 1971 Census and other sources). The figures are in chapter 2.

I have generalized (with caution) from the case of four factories, and from a small sample of workers. All four factories are capital intensive and use fairly advanced technologies; but there are wide

---

[7] See M. Holmström, 'Action-sets and ideology: a municipal election in South India', *Contributions to Indian Sociology*, new series, 3 (1969), 76–93; 'Religious change in an industrial city of South India', *Journal of the Royal Asiatic Society*, (1971), no. 1, 28–40; and 'Caste and status in an Indian city', *Economic and Political Weekly*, 8 April 1972, 769–74.

variations in work processes and the routine of factory life, from repetitive assembly-line work to one-off jobs by craftsmen working to specifications. These men are a fair sample of the work force in the 'organized' sector. Numerically this is a small part of India's population: but it is likely to grow as high-technology industries expand – especially into export markets – even if the main emphasis of industrialization shifts towards smaller units with simpler technology (and, as I have suggested, it is doubtful whether a big shift in this direction is possible or likely). The present industrial workers are strategically important as a nucleus of skilled people; and they have an economic multiplier effect because of the number of service workers, unemployed, and poorer relatives in rural areas whom they support directly or indirectly.

Thus the study does not attempt to draw conclusions about the whole Indian industrial work force, but to fit an important strategic section of it into the sociological understanding we already have of Indian society – especially rural society, from which all the best ethnography has come.

Anthropological approaches to industrial society

Since the pioneering work of M. N. Srinivas in the 1940s, Indian social anthropology has produced some remarkable studies of rural and small-town society (I use these terms to avoid the loaded and misleading 'traditional society'). These have given us useful and testable hypotheses about caste, the family, economic changes, religion, politics and so on. But the anthropology of the new occupations and the large towns (which is not new in the West or Japan) has been patchy an uncertain of its methods, in spite of a few excellent pioneering works.[8]

One way of using anthropological methods in an industrial situation is to take the factory as a more or less closed system of relations, like the 'little community' of (allegedly) 'classical' anthropology. But this is inadequate, partly because relations inside the factory have very different meanings and importance for workers at different levels of skill, at different stages in the career, with different values, intentions for the future, and life chances. One man con-

[8] In particular, Lambert, *Workers, factories and social change*; K. M. Kapadia and S. Devadas Pillai, *Industrialization and rural society* (Bombay, 1972); N. R. Sheth, *The social framework of an Indian factory* (Manchester, 1968); O. Lynch, *The politics of untouchability* (New York, 1969); and A. Niehoff, *Factory workers in India* (Milwaukee, 1959).

centrates all his efforts (realistically or hopefully) on advancing his career in one factory; another clings to his job as his only resource, or to his fellow workers as his only friends and allies; another takes the job for granted, and the projects which matter most to him do not concern his working life at all; another sees factory work as a stage before he will go on to something quite different; and so on.

I have tried to place these people in their whole working and social environment: structured, to begin with, as they see it, and using their categories and distinctions as my point of departure. Their points of contact *with each other* are the factory and institutions connected with it (like the union). This makes the factory a convenient unit for study, rather than a self-conscious or closed group.[9] A minority (in my sample, only some workers in the two public sector factories) also live in factory townships – built, rented out, serviced and policed by the management. The others live in rented accommodation in neighbourhoods inhabited by all kinds of people, mainly by workers in factories and 'unorganized sector' workshops, in this sprawling industrial city. These areas where factory workers live have something of a common culture, so that one can talk of a characteristic Indian industrial society.

Chapter 2 gives a background of factual, statistical and 'macro-' information about this society. Chapter 3 brings together what workers say and information from other sources, in a discussion of workers' backgrounds, home life, recruitment, career patterns, intentions for the future etc. Chapter 4 contains commented summaries of some case studies – workers' own accounts of their life histories, and ideas about their situation now – grouped for convenience into a number of types of social outlook and situation; chapter 5 is an experiment in analysing and comparing the structures of a career and a lifetime, seen from these different points of view. Chapter 6 offers tentative answers to the three questions which are the focus of this study, some thoughts on industrialization, and suggestions for further research.

[9] It is arguable that a functionalist and positivist bias has led rural anthropologists to look for closed and balanced systems of relations (sanctions and rewards etc.) and then to invent theories of 'social change' to cope with extraneous facts which could not be fitted into the model (as if there could be a sociology which is *not* a theory of social change). The shortcomings of this approach are less obvious (though not less real) when one is dealing with physically isolated rural communities. In cities there are only networks of relations, overlapping groups, conflicts not only of obligations but of ideals and ideas: a more open, dialectical approach (which would also explain the facts of rural life better) is the *only* way to make sense of urban society.

2

Bangalore and its factory workers

Bangalore, the capital of Mysore State,[1] lies on the Deccan plateau at an altitude of 900 metres, 350 kilometres west of Madras and about the same distance east of Mangalore on the Arabian Sea.

The city was founded in the sixteenth century. In the nineteenth century the British built a Cantonment, or Civil and Military Station, outside the old town, with broad avenues, rambling bungalows, italianate or gothic churches, and parks (once Churchill, who was once stationed there, called it 'a dreary watering place'). This Cantonment was governed as part of 'British India', and a town grew up around it. The old city was in the dominions of the Maharaja of Mysore, who made it his capital. The two halves of Bangalore were merged under a single municipal corporation after Independence in 1947. Both the old city and the Cantonment, like many surrounding villages, have been swallowed up in the rapid growth of Bangalore since then.

Before the British conquest, Bangalore was already one of the chief manufacturing and trading towns of South India, making handloom textiles, carpets and luxury goods. The first powered factories were two textile mills founded in the 1880s, in the Maharaja's part of the city. From then on the state government, under a succession of enlightened Dewans (prime ministers), gave financial and practical support to new industries, and planned to follow the example of the Japanese Meiji government by setting up state factories and selling them off when they become going concerns. Thus the government started factories making soap, porcelain, light-bulbs and transformers: but it made no serious efforts to sell them. In the 1920s, the state established a polytechnic to teach mechanical skills and science. By 1939 Bangalore had three large textile mills and a range of smaller factories, but nothing to compare with industrial giants like Ahmedabad and Jamshedpur. It was a commercial, administrative and garrison town: sleepy and pleasant, known as the 'garden city' or 'pensioners' paradise'.

[1] The name has since been changed to Karnataka. Mysore is the name of the former princely state and the old capital. Since it was the state's official name at the time of my fieldwork, I use it here.

Bangalore and its factory workers

Bangalore had few natural advantages except its central position in South India and its climate, which made it possible to work hard throughout the year, and attracted skilled Indian and foreign staff. But it had exceptional man-made economies: hydro-electric power, roads and railways, a relatively high standard of education and a supply of skilled or educated labour. Its present industrial expansion began with the foundation of the Hindustan Aircraft factory in 1940. After the Second World War the central government and private business realized Bangalore's industrial potential, and for some fifteen years the town's industry and population increased rapidly. In the decade 1941–51, the population of Bangalore Metropolitan Area increased by 91 per cent, from 410 967 to 786 343, largely because of immigration from the neighbouring state of Madras (now Tamil Nadu). From 1951 to 1961, it grew by 53 per cent; from 1961 to 1971, by a further 43 per cent. With a population of 1 653 779 (1971 Census), Bangalore is India's sixth largest city.

The largest factories make aircraft, telephones, machine tools, watches, electrical and electronic equipment, and earth movers. The state government has its pre-war factories, and a larger post-war factory making electrical switchgear. The main private industries are five textile mills, and factories making car components, cigarettes, electric motors and transformers. Smaller private factories make components for the large public sector factories, as well as batteries, liquid oxygen, tin cans, canned fruits and a wide range of engineering and consumer goods. A large number of small engineering and other workshops are regarded as being outside the 'organized sector', since each firm employs (officially) less than ten workers and is not affected by legislation on social security, dismissals, inspection, and trade-union rights. A number of research institutes (like the prestigious Indian Institute of Science) are established in the city. As Nehru said on a visit, 'Bangalore is very much a picture of India of the future, more especially because of the concentration of science, technology and industries in the public sector here.'

Import controls give Bangalore's engineering, electronic and consumer-goods industries an assured market for almost all they produce; and Bangalore remains a most attractive location for new private or public sector investments because of its external economies, especially skilled labour. All 'organized sector' factories have to take a quota of apprentices, though not necessarily to employ them afterwards; and the training sections in public sector factories are intended not only to meet the factories' own needs, but to train workers who will find work elsewhere. A government Industrial Training Institute prepares students without cost for certificates in mechanical or

9

electrical engineering. Many private institutes prepare fee-paying students for similar certificates or diplomas, and for qualifications in textile technology, automobile engineering, typing, shorthand etc. Smaller engineering workshops give less formal training to 'helpers', who may be employed as semi-casual workers on very low wages. Since there are more trained people than jobs, there is a constant surplus of educated unemployed, with technical training in skills no longer in demand; yet other skilled workers and technicians are attracted to Bangalore by the opportunities in new or expanding firms, and by the city's climate and other advantages.

The expansion continues: at the time of my fieldwork it was gathering momentum after the depression of the mid 1960s. One reason for this expansion was the influx of private capital from Calcutta, affected by the naxalite violence, and of Indian businessmen forced out of East Africa. Under the headline 'One new industry every month', the *Indian Express* (Bangalore, 1 Nov. 1971) reported that the central government had licenced a number of private industries, including a tractor plant, other engineering works and two cigarette factories, to open within the next few months; with several large units already commissioned, the article continued, 'Bangalore can happily look forward to another big phase of industrial expansion. In fact, it never had it so good.' New licence applications were coming in, including several for factories to make television sets; the existing public sector firms were installing new plants to make helicopters and automatic wrist watches. (Since then, of course, Bangalore has been hit by the national economic crisis, caused by world-wide inflation and especially the rise in oil prices.)

This is the background to the careers of the men this book is about. There is some (not enough) statistical evidence to show how representative these men are of the 'organized sector' work force in Bangalore; how this work force compares with the rest of the population; and how the situation in Bangalore compares with that in the rest of the country.

Bangalore, Mysore State and the rest of India

Mysore State, or Karnataka, with 29.3 million people, has 5.35 per cent of India's population. The population of Bangalore, the state capital, was 1 653 779 in 1971.[2] The urban population of Bangalore

[2] This figure is for the Bangalore Urban Agglomeration; from the *Census of India 1971: Paper 1 of 1972: Final population* (Delhi, 1972).

District (i.e. the city and surrounding smaller towns) was 1 865 754.
The sex ratio for Mysore State was 957 (females/1000 males),
a little above the national ratio (932). The sex ratio for Bangalore
was 834, slightly below the national urban ratio (859),[3] but well above
that for many large cities in the north: in 1961 the ratio for Bombay
was only 596. For generations the large northern cities have had a
large excess of males, made up of unmarried immigrants or men who
leave families in rural areas, and return only for holidays and festivals.
But the typical South Indian immigrant takes his family with him,
or brings them to town as soon as he finds somewhere to live.[4] However, Bangalore's sex ratio in 1971 (834) was a little lower than in 1961
(874). Evidently many immigrants to Bangalore over the past ten
years have been bachelor workers: my case study sample contains
many of them. One district of Mysore State (South Kanara) had an
excess of females (sex ratio 1 061), which was attributed to emigration by men seeking work in distant cities: I knew some of them.

Mysore's literacy rate (32 per cent of the total population) and
female literacy rate (20 per cent) were slightly above the national
averages in 1971 (29 and 18 per cent) but well below the regional
average (39 per cent literacy, and 27 per cent female literacy, in
Tamil Nadu; 60 and 54 per cent in Kerala). Bangalore had 59 per
cent literacy and 50 per cent female literacy (59 and 49 per cent in
the urban population of Bangalore District), which is high for India,
and has been high for a long time.[5]

Of Mysore State's population 24 per cent are 'urban', compared
with 20 per cent for the whole country. Bangalore, the capital, is by
far the biggest town; the next, Hubli-Dharwar, has 379 166 people,
and there are another nine towns of over 100 000. Bangalore grew
by 43 per cent in the years 1961–71 (and is now four times as large
as in 1941); but several of these smaller towns have grown faster.
Another 220 towns have populations of between 10 000 and 100 000.

Mysore State has slightly more 'workers' (35.2 per cent of the
population) than the national average (33.5); and a higher proportion
of Mysore workers are 'other workers', i.e. not agricultural (34.6

[3] *Census of India 1971: Paper 1 of 1971: Provisional population totals* (Delhi, 1971).
[4] 'The cities of the South ... generally show a stabler state of society as reflected
in a fairly balanced sex ratio' (*ibid.* p. 20). I do not know why this is so: perhaps
because of the high proportion of landless labourers in the south, who had no need
to leave their families looking after the farm.
[5] 'There seems to be a concentration of the more literate cities in the South'
(*ibid.* p. 21). India's four most literate cities are in Kerala, and the next two are
in Tamil Nadu.

per cent, cf. 31.4 for all India).[6] Thirty per cent of Bangalore people are workers. In 1968, 756 000 people in the state were counted as 'employed', two-thirds of them in the public sector;[7] but the real number working in the private sector was probably much higher.

By 1970 Bangalore had 3 422 'organized sector' factories, covered by the Factories Act,[8] with an estimated average daily employment of 260 000, or 5.4 per cent of the national total (about the same as the state's share of India's population); the 1961 figure was only 4.5 per cent of the national total.

Factories in Mysore State employ many more women than the national average: 15 per cent of total employment in factories submitting returns in 1971, as against 9 per cent for all India.

With a per capita income of Rs 629, Mysore came seventh among the sixteen states in the period 1967–8; but the annual growth of real income since 1960 was high at 4 per cent, equal to Gujarat and behind only Punjab and Haryana (5 per cent; the rate for Uttar Pradesh – the most populous state – was 0.5 per cent).[9] But the annual money earnings of workers in manufacturing industries in Mysore were well below the national average in 1961 (Rs 1375, or 89 per cent of the national figure), still further below it in 1970 (Rs 2088, or 79 per cent).[10] Over this period the real value of Indian factory workers' earnings fell by 2 per cent.

'Organized' and 'unorganized sector' industries in Bangalore

Factories in the 'organized sector' are those which employ ten or more workers.[11] They are covered by factory legislation on wages,

[6] *Indian labour statistics 1972* (Delhi, 1972), based on the 1971 Census. A worker is 'a person whose main activity is participation in any economically productive work by his physical or mental activity'. Previous censuses took secondary activities into account.

[7] *Indian labour year book 1968* (Delhi, 1971).

[8] *Indian labour statistics 1972*. A factory is covered by the Act if it employs ten or more workers (except seasonally) and uses power; or employs twenty or more workers without power; or has been brought under the Act by another act of the state government. The figures include some clerical and supervisory staff, and estimates for factories not submitting returns; but I suspect many small establishments, which should be covered by the Act, have not been counted.

[9] B. N. Ganguli, in A. J. Fonseca (ed.), *Challenge of poverty in India* (Delhi, 1971), p. 13.

[10] *Indian labour statistics 1972*. Earnings include bonuses and the value of concessions. Workers earning over Rs 400 a month in 1971 (previously Rs 200) are excluded: this may make the Mysore figures too low, if many highly skilled workers (especially in Bangalore) have been left out.

[11] For twenty, if the factory does not use power (see footnote 8, above). The Act

hours and conditions of work, safety and hygiene, union recognition and Employees' State Insurance. The laws governing conditions in the 'unorganized sector' are often evaded.[12] A statistical profile of the two sectors in Bangalore has to be patched together from figures which are not quite comparable, because they refer to different dates or definitions, and because it is hard to collect accurate statistics on the 'unorganized sector'. The latest figures for workers in different 'industrial categories' are given in table 1. In 1961 Bangalore had a higher ratio of industrial workers to all workers, and to the

TABLE I. *Population of Bangalore Urban Agglomeration, by work, 1971*
(total population: 1 653 779)

Industrial category	Males (%)	Females (%)	Total (%)
Cultivators	0.3	–	0.2
Agricultural labourers	0.3	0.1	0.2
Livestock, forestry, fishing, hunting, plantations, orchards and allied activities	0.3	0.1	0.2
Mining and quarrying	–	–	–
Manufacturing, processing, servicing and repairs			
– Household industry	1.2	0.3	0.8
– Other than household industry	17.2	1.4	9.8
Construction	2.3	0.3	1.4
Trade and commerce	9.6	0.6	5.4
Transport, storage and communications	6.1	0.8	3.6
Other services	12.0	3.2	7.9
Total workers	49.3	6.8	29.5
Non-workers	50.7	93.2	70.5

SOURCE: *Census of India 1971*, Series 14, *Mysore, Part II–A: General population tables* (Delhi, 1973), pp. 320f.

is widely evaded by owners of small workshops, who employ illegal child labour, and/or split a single workshop – sometimes by a sign in the middle of the shed – into two fictitious firms, each employing not more than ten workers (see *Report of the National Commission on Labour* (Delhi, 1969), p. 36).

[12] This is because of the difficulty of enforcement rather than a lack of official effort. Thus child labour (though not by *very* young children) is quite common in the 'unorganized sector', in spite of genuine attempts to enforce the constitutional ban on employing any child under 14 in a factory, mine or other hazardous occupation.

whole population, than any of the five larger cities except Bombay (see table 2).

About 44 per cent of workers in Bangalore District seem to be employed in the organized sector.[13] Since part of the District is rural, the figure may be higher in the city of Bangalore: perhaps 50 per cent. Of organized sector workers 71 per cent (compared to 31 per cent of all workers) are employed in the public sector; 10 per cent are women. Table 3 shows that 51 per cent of organized sector workers are in manufacturing industry.

This leaves about half Bangalore's workers unaccounted for. They are in the 'unorganized sector', which includes most 'small' (or 'small-scale') industries,[14] almost all 'cottage industries', a mass of small

TABLE 2. *Industrial workers in India's six largest cities, 1961*

City	Population	Industrial workers as a percentage of all workers	Industrial workers as a percentage of population
Greater Bombay	4 152 056	40.8	16.6
Calcutta[a]	2 927 289	26.0	10.5
Delhi	2 359 408	22.5	7.1
Madras	1 729 141	27.0	8.2
Hyderabad	1 251 119	19.7	5.9
Bangalore Metropolitan Area	1 206 961	34.6	11.2

SOURCE: Government of Mysore, *Outline development plan for the Bangalore Metropolitan Region* (Bangalore, 1968), p. 17. Evidently the definition of 'industry' is narrower here than for table 1.

These figures must be treated with caution, because of the difficulty of enumerating the 'unorganized sector' work force, but the differences between cities should be about right.

[a] But Calcutta Metropolitan District had a population of about 6 580 000, making it the largest city.

[13] This figure was arrived at indirectly: the census gives the working population of the District as 30 per cent, which is about 558 000. The Bangalore Sub-Regional Labour Exchange's *Annual area employment market information report, period ending 31.3.1972* (Bangalore, 1972) estimates organized sector employment at 247 304 on 31 March 1971, a month after the census was taken. The other figures in this paragraph, except the estimate for 'all workers', are from the same report.

[14] A great deal of official effort is devoted to stimulating 'small(-scale) industries', e.g. through the Small Industries Service Institutes, which provide finishing workshops, training and other facilities in Bangalore and other large towns.

TABLE 3.   *Organized sector employment in Bangalore District, by industry, 1971*

Industry	Public sector employment	Private sector employment	Total employment	Total as a percentage of organized sector employment
Agriculture, forestry and livestock	1 492	—	1 492	0.6
Manufacturing	71 452	54 486	125 938	51.0
Construction	3 834	156	3 980	1.6
Electricity, gas and water-supply services	3 503	122	3 625	1.5
Trade and commerce	10 352	4 534	14 886	6.0
Transport, storage and communications	12 146	1 000	13 146	5.3
Services	72 659	11 578	84 237	34.0

SOURCE: Based on the same market information report (see footnote 13, p. 14), which uses 'information received from all employers in the Public Sector and those employing 10 persons and above in the Private Sector excluding Agriculture'. Clearly many private employers (especially in construction) gave no figures. Detailed census figures are not yet available.

non-industrial establishments like shops, and people working on their own account. I have no up-to-date figures for shops, cafés (called 'hotels' in India) and other very small firms: I doubt whether anything better than an informed guess is possible, since many small employers or partnerships must be outside any system of registration, and may be missed by the census and the National Sample Survey.

'Small industries' is a misnomer: these are really small *enterprises*, which in places like Bangalore are often interdependent parts of industries organized on a large scale (e.g. suppliers of components to factories). See P. N. Dhar and H. F. Lydall, *The role of small enterprises in Indian economic development* (Bombay, 1961), p. 1.

A firm is in the 'organized sector' if it employs (officially) more than ten workers. Most definitions of 'smallness' emphasize investment rather than labour force: thus T. K. Lakshman (*Cottage and small-scale industries in Mysore* (Mysore, 1966), p. 4) regards a firm as small if its investment is under 5 lakhs (500 000 rupees).

15

A very large number of people work for building and public works contractors: for example, whole families of casual workers, who break granite in stone quarries in and around the city for road-making. Those working on their own account include many, chiefly women, who make agarbathis or incense sticks at home – this is something of a Mysore speciality – and sell them to the merchants who provide the raw materials (see Lakshman, pp. 187ff.): I believe a hard worker could hope to make 4 000 agarbathis a day at a profit of Rs 3. Other women sell hot snacks at the doors of their houses. Both sexes in the urban villages keep cows and sell the milk locally or to the city dairies. Men, with a minimum of training, drive autorikshas for owners who pay them according to the distance driven, and some have their own vehicles. The Commissioner of Labour in Mysore made these rough estimates of the numbers of persons working on their own account in some of these occupations (1972):

	Males	Females	Total
Autoriksha drivers	6 000	–	6 000
Street vendors	3 500	1 000	4 500
Market porters	10 500	200	10 700
Agarbathi makers	1 837	1 000	2 837

So these four occupations (all except autoriksha driving poorly paid) account for 24 000 workers, perhaps a twelfth of the unorganized sector.

The part of the unorganized sector that is most closely connected with the organized sector consists of the many small engineering workshops scattered throughout the city, especially in industrial suburbs near larger factories and industrial estates. Lakshman's pioneering study, *Cottage and small-scale industries in Mysore* (pp. 201f.), describes their organization, techniques and markets in some detail:

Small-scale engineering industries . . . are distinct from cottage industries in their productive process which is highly rationalized utilizing more specialized machines, and employ skilled workers. It is these features along with their ability and willingness to adapt themselves to demand, that have enabled them to stand up to the competition from the organized sector . . .

They are mainly concentrated around Bangalore largely because of the availability of skilled labourers, trained either in a factory or under a master mechanic of a small workshop. Secondly, the existence of large industries such as textiles and automobiles in the same area has created a market for the products of engineering units.[15] Further, Bangalore being a growing commercial and industrial centre, the demand for the products of the small industries has been increasing considerably.

Before the Second World War, Bangalore had only half-a-dozen establishments, many of which manufactured spare parts of machines and later on whole machines. In the initial stages, their capital equipment consisted of heavy machinery largely imported. The Second World War created a scarcity of heavy machinery and their spare parts, while, at the same time, the war needs increased the demand for consumer goods. This led to a number of skilled workers employed in various organized establishments starting independent small units. The easy money created due to inflationary conditions facilitated the organization of these units, many of which were built out of scrap. Simultaneously, the unskilled apprentices were mobilized and trained so that in the course of the two decades following the war, different units of various sizes manufacturing different kinds of machinery and spare parts could spring up.

In 1961 Mysore State had 11 826 'establishments making machinery and electrical equipment, transport equipment and miscellaneous manufacturing industries'; 97 per cent of them employed less than ten workers, and 67 per cent were in urban areas. Lakshman took a sample of 112 small engineering units (with an investment of under 5 lakhs), of which over half were in Bangalore. Over half the sample (63) were machine shops, with an average of ten workers, engaged largely in filing and machining rough castings to make machine parts. Most machine shops have lathes, and often drilling and grinding machines. 'The entrepreneur is himself a skilled worker and employs, in addition, skilled and semi-skilled labourers and also a few apprentices' (p. 224). Other small engineering establishments are foundries, with 'low quality output, high costs of production owing to inferior technique, keen competition and limited market largely confining [*sic*] to the local area' (p. 211). These foundries employ on average six workers, including one or two skilled men.

The remaining firms are 'machine-shop-cum-foundries', mostly in Bangalore. A 'machine-shop-cum-foundry' is usually run by an entrepreneur who is himself a skilled worker, relatively quality-conscious, capable of improving and even inventing machinery, and

---

[15] The reference to 'automobiles' must mean car parts (springs, spark plugs etc.) made in Bangalore for assembly elsewhere.

anxious to learn new techniques. Most of his employees are skilled men, and, as Lakshman says, 'these skilled labourers have a shrewd sense of practical engineering and are capable of learning up-to-date methods under proper training and guidance' (p. 234). They are paid only for the days worked – normally twenty-five days a month – and tend to leave as soon as they get regular employment in one of the large factories.

Small engineering units in general suffer from raw material shortages, lack of skilled management, low productivity because of worn-out machinery and obsolete techniques, and severe problems of finance and marketing. The workers are not trained systematically; their work is 'a crude imitation of the work of a skilled worker'. They have low wages and no security of employment, pensions, leave, or maternity benefits. 'This low wage and the absence of social security measures are chiefly because of the marginal existence of many small undertakings, low productivity per worker, low rate of profit and the absence of any organization of the workers' (p. 367).[16]

The four sample factories

I shall call the sample factories A and B (public sector), C and D (private), in order of their size (see table 4). How typical are they of organized sector industry in Bangalore?

Factories A and B are large, but not the biggest in Bangalore. Public sector factories are generally much bigger than private ones, except for one private textile mill. All four are post-war, like most Bangalore factories. The public sector ones were founded fifteen to twenty years ago, while the private ones were only eight and ten years old. Again, this fits the Bangalore pattern, since the post-war foundation of giant public enterprises stimulated the growth of smaller private ones. All four, like many Bangalore factories, use technical processes as advanced as any in India, and require high levels of skill. There is also room for a number of semi-skilled (but educated) workers, and a few unskilled.

The private factories pay better. Public sector wages are standardized, though not rigidly, to discourage movement of skilled labour between factories. Well-equipped modern private factories like C and

[16] It is fair to add that official and academic interest in the problems of small firms (Lakshman's book is an example) has led to stronger government action to deal with these problems – especially through Small Industries Service Institutes, and buying policies designed to give small firms a steady market for components needed by public sector factories.

18

TABLE 4. *The four sample factories*

Factory	Public or private sector	Work force[a]	Percentage of women workers	Sampling fraction (%) (random sample)[b]	Number in random sample	Number in case study sample
A	Public	14 000	5.1	2.8	389	23
B	Public	5 200	1.7	6.8	353	26
C	Private	650	34.6	20.0	130	22
D	Private	524	9.5	50.0	262	33
Total		20 374	8.5	5.6	1134	104

[a] The definition of 'work force' varies between factories. Usually it includes most office staff and some supervisory staff. The figures for factories A and B are rough, because of anomalies in reckoning the totals taken from different sources.

[b] Unstratified systematic random sample, i.e. every *n*th file or roll number. In factories A and B, the assistants who helped me with the statistical work tried to take 2 and 5%, until we found that many workers selected from the original list were no longer on the payroll.

D can offer high wages to attract skilled labour, and assured markets give them some flexibility in facing union demands. These two are among the best payers in Bangalore.

In three of the four factories, the percentage of women is well below the average for factories in the state (15 per cent). This may be because some of the work in these factories involves heavy machinery. Other Bangalore factories tend to employ women for repetitive assembly-line work, apart from a relatively small number in office jobs (as steno-typists etc.), for which they compete with men. In one sample factory only (C), one-third of the work force are women – mostly on assembly-line work. South Indian city women are not secluded and will readily join in conversation in a mixed group, but detailed interviews with women were hard to arrange: there is only one in my case study sample.

How typical is the case study sample of the work force in the four factories?

This book is based on case studies of 104 workers from the four factories: 49 workers in public sector factories, 55 in the private sector. A random sample of the files, which managements keep on each worker, shows how far I succeeded in selecting a typical cross-section of the work force from those to whom I had personal introductions from other workers.

The most useful part of each file is a card giving the worker's age, marital status, record of training and promotions and so on. Other details (religion, caste, language) can often be found out from other papers in the file, e.g. the letter applying for the job.

The two private sector factories (C and D) were eight and ten years old, and the workers' median age in both was 27. In the older public sector factories, the median ages were 34 and 35. The case study sample was typical of the age distribution in all factories, except that I had a younger sample in factory A (see table 5). The median length of service was only five and three years in the private factories (because of recent expansion), ten and eleven years in the others. The case study sample workers had rather longer service (see table 6).

Differences in basic pay do not reflect the real differences between

TABLE 5. *Workers in the four factories, by age (both samples)*

Age	Percentage of workers from each factory in each 5-year age range (random sample)				Whole random sample
	Factory A	Factory B	Factory C	Factory D	
15–19	—	—	1	3	1
20–4	6	3	23	27	12
25–9	27	12	48	42	28
30–4	20	30	15	22	23
35–9	22	28	9	5	18
40–4	14	16	2	—	10
45–9	8	5	2	—	5
50–4	2	4	—	—	2
55–9	1	1	—	—	1
Median age in random sample	34	35	27	27	31
Median age in case study sample	31	36	27	27	29
Difference between the random and case study samples	−3	+1	0	0	−2

NOTE: In this table (and most others) percentages have been rounded off to the nearest 1%.

TABLE 6. *Years of service in present factory (both samples)*

	Factory A	Factory B	Factory C	Factory D	The four factories
Median (random sample)	10	11	5	3	8
Median (case study) sample)	11	$12\frac{1}{2}$	7	8	$8\frac{1}{2}$
Difference	+1	$+1\frac{1}{2}$	+2	+5	$+\frac{1}{2}$

earnings in different factories, because of overtime and because of wide variations in Dearness Allowance (DA), bonus and fringe benefits, and in the seniority and skill of work forces. The big private factories in Bangalore certainly pay more (I think about 20 per cent more) than the public sector. Within each factory, differences in basic pay are more closely related to take-home pay. There are no reliable or comparable figures for earnings in the unorganized sector: all one can say with confidence is that organized sector workers earn much more than most workers in the unorganized sector.

In each factory studied, the median salary of the case study sample

TABLE 7. *Basic salaries in rupees (both samples)*

	Factory A	Factory B	Factory C	Factory D
Random sample				
Low quartile	145	195	135	125
Median	175	235	185	175
High quartile	215	245	205	215
Semi-interquartile range	35	25	35	45
Case study sample				
Low quartile	150	230	160	205
Median	180	245	200	270
High quartile	220	285	210	380
Semi-interquartile range	35	27.50	25	87.50
Difference between the medians (case study sample minus random sample)	5	10	15	95

NOTE: Basic salaries are not comparable between factories.

was slightly above that of the random sample, as table 7 shows. This can easily be explained by longer service, since most workers get automatic annual pay rises and seniority is the main criterion for promotion to a higher grade. There is a marked difference between the random and case study samples in factory D, where the case study sample earn much more than the random sample. I now think the contacts I used in this factory were too restricted and middle class. Of course, the educated, skilled and better-paid workers are more articulate and easier to contact; I tried to guard against this distortion, and now I must allow for it.

Over half the workers in the four factories (52 per cent) had a Senior School Leaving Certificate (SSLC, now the minimum qualification for most factory jobs) or better; many of the others had failed SSLC (see table 8). But 64 per cent of the case study sample had SSLC or better; again, this shows I had a better educated and more articulate sample – especially in the two older public sector factories (A and B), which recruited many of their present workers when there was not the present intense competition among high-school leavers for factory work. But in both samples the great majority of men had reached high school (72 per cent in the random sample, 84 per cent in the case study sample). And a higher proportion of the case study sample have some formal technical qualification (40.4 per cent, cf. 25.5 per cent of the random sample: see table 9).

There are 83 per cent Hindu workers in the four factories, 14 per cent Christians (Bangalore has a large Christian population) and 3 per cent Muslims (see table 10); 15 per cent of workers are Scheduled Caste Hindus (i.e. Harijans or ex-'Untouchables'; see table 11). There are probably more Scheduled Caste workers in the public sector factories, which have to take a quota; and more Christians in the private sector. Scheduled Caste workers earn rather less than the others, because more of them are in menial or unskilled jobs. The figures show that I included too few Scheduled Caste workers in the case study sample (7 per cent), though I tried to get a fair sample of the whole work force. (Table 15, p. 32, shows the castes and religions of the case study sample in detail.)

The figures in table 12 show that 42 per cent of workers in the four factories speak Kannad'a, the majority language in Mysore State, as their first language. And 26 per cent speak Tamil, the language of the neighbouring state of Tamil Nadu (formerly Madras). Many of these Tamils are Bangalore-born; Tamils have been the largest single language group in Bangalore since the nineteenth century. (There is now a militant movement to reserve jobs for Kannad'igas, and to

TABLE 8. *General education (both samples)*

Education	Random sample					
	Factory A (%)	Factory B (%)	Factory C (%)	Factory D (%)	Whole random sample (%)	Case study sample (%)
No formal education	6	6	4	6	6	–
Primary (below Standard V)	10	13	7	1	8	–
Middle school (Standard V–VI)	9	7	6	3	7	2
Middle school (Standard VII–VIII)	4	12	9	6	7	10
High school (Standard IX–XII, including failed SSLC/Matric)	15	20	25	25	20	20
SSLC/Matric (passed)	41	31	41	49	40	48
PUC (Pre-University or Intermediate)	9	7	4	5	7	14
Graduates	6	6	5	5	6	1
Not known (i.e. mostly with little or no education)	–	–	–	–	–	5
Total with SSLC or better	56	43	50	59	52	64

exclude even Mysore-born Tamils; see pp. 36–8.) Tamils tend to earn a little more than Kannadigas.

Altogether 73 per cent of the work force were born in Mysore State, and only 13 per cent in Tamil Nadu (see table 13). The case study was fairly representative by state of birth, but contained too many

TABLE 9. *Formal technical qualifications (both samples)*

Technical qualification	Random sample				Whole random sample (%)	Case study sample (%)
	Factory A (%)	Factory B (%)	Factory C (%)	Factory D (%)		
Industrial Training Institute course (18 months)	8.5	10.5	1.6	2.3	6.9	10.1
Apprenticeship (at least 2 years)	–	0.6	0.8	2.3	0.8	6.1
Ex-Craftsman Trainee, or Diploma in Craftsmanship (course lasts 18 months or more)	–	0.6	0.8	0.4	0.4	1.0
Diploma in Engineering, Licentiate in Engineering, or comparable Diploma	10.0	9.1	6.3	6.3	8.4	7.1
Other certificate (including typing etc.)	7.7	10.5	5.5	10.5	9.0	16.2
Any technical qualification	26.2	31.4	14.8	21.9	25.5	40.4
No technical qualification	73.8	68.6	85.2	78.1	74.5	59.6

NOTE: All figures are rounded off to 0.1%.

Tamils and too few Kannad'a speakers (partly because I speak Tamil better than Kannad'a).[17]

The figures which follow refer to the case study sample only. The

[17] Many interviews with workers were in English, which most of them know and use at work: the situation here is very different from that in North India. Sometimes I interviewed them in Tamil, or in Kannad'a with the help of people standing around; and I talked to their families mainly in Tamil or Kannad'a.

The case study sample: typical of the work force?

TABLE 10. *Religion (both samples, and Bangalore in 1961)*

Religion	Random sample (%)	Case study sample (%)	Bangalore District (urban population), 1961 (%)[a]
Hindu	83	75	78
Christian	14	19	7
Muslim	3	5	14
Other	0 +	1	1

[a] SOURCE: *Census of India 1961: Paper 1 of 1963: 1961 Census – Religion* (Delhi, 1967).

TABLE 11. *Scheduled Castes (Harijans) (both samples, and Bangalore in 1971)*

In the four factories (random sample)	15%
In case study sample	7
In Bangalore	10

NOTE: In public sector firms the files show whether a worker is Scheduled Caste. In private ones it can usually be found out by examining the application for employment, since private firms are under official pressure to recruit Harijans and a Harijan applicant will often mention his caste in his application.

TABLE 12. *Language (both samples, and Bangalore)*

Language	Random sample (%)	Case study sample (%)	Bangalore, 1952 (%)[a]
Kannad'a	42	26	22
Tamil	26	36	36
Telugu	16	15	18
Hindi or Urdu	4	6	15
Malayalam	6	8	
Marathi	3	1	
Kokani	1	5	9
English (mainly Anglo-Indians)	0.4	2	
Others	1	2	

[a] SOURCE: UN, *Mysore population study* (Calcutta, 1961), p. 57. I have not been able to find more recent figures: the percentage of Kannad'a speakers is certainly higher now. In the 1961 Census the figures for Bangalore *District* (including rural areas) were: 51% Kannad'a, 17% Telugu, 16% Tamil and 11% Urdu or Hindi.

TABLE 13. *State of birth (both samples)*

State of birth	Random sample (%)	Case study sample (%)
Mysore State (Karnataka)	73	64
Tamil Nadu (formerly Madras)	13	14
Andhra Pradesh	6	10
Kerala	7	8
Maharashtra	1	–
Goa	–	2
Elsewhere in India	1	1
Pakistan (present territory)	0.3	–
Elsewhere abroad	0.5	1

median household has 5 members. In workers' households, there are two non-workers to each (earning) worker. The sample has 37 per cent unmarried workers; 44 per cent live in households consisting of more than a nuclear family. Trainees – and, in two factories, supervisors – are not eligible to join unions; 96% of the others do so. The case study sample includes a high proportion of enthusiastic union members and present or past office-holders, because I used the unions to make contacts.

These are the basic (and inadequate) figures. The 104 workers in the case study sample are not too untypical of the work force in the four factories studied. There is some bias towards the more educated, skilled and articulate workers (especially in factory A), but this bias has been quantified and can be allowed for. The four factories' work force is a fair sample of that in post-war 'organized sector' factories in Bangalore and similar towns, where industrial expansion is recent and based on advanced technology.

These people's situation has to be seen against the background of a large 'unorganized sector' in urban industry and services, offering (generally) lower incomes, no security, bad working conditions, but more employment now; and against the much larger background of rural poverty.

But Indian urban and rural society are not two watertight compartments, in terms of social relations or economic structure. In the next chapter I trace some of the connexions. The practical problems of the countryside are different, but their solution may depend largely on the development of a diversified industrial economy in cities like Bangalore.

3

Life as a factory worker

These factory workers have much in common. They belong to a distinctive Indian industrial culture, with typical assumptions and expectations and tastes which cut across divisions of skill and age and origin. They share a common situation. They act, and sometimes think of themselves, as a group (if not a class) different from peasants, workers in the 'unorganized sector' or in older factories with different technologies, from casual labourers, shopkeepers, professional people and so on. I would need the skill of a novelist like R. K. Narayan to give the real flavour of their life and company.

This chapter brings together individual workers' accounts of their careers, and what else I know about their situation and chances, to build up a composite picture of what it is to be an organized sector worker now, matching 'facts' and workers' arguments in particular contexts of experience – like job finding, home life and so on.

What is happening to these people? How do they and others see their situation, and make sense of it in terms of the value-loaded categories they already have (the self in relation to others, castes, classes, marriage, career etc.)? How do they act to achieve existing objectives (the 'logic of the situation')? How do they revise social categories and values, and set themselves new objectives, taking into account a new situation and the choices it presents them with?

This approach to the dialectic of situation, thought and action implies that the agent chooses freely, that he constructs his own world, within the constraints of real possibilities, available knowledge and so on. This construction is a creative act, neither random nor wholly determined: the limits of social determination cannot be known or assumed in advance, but have to be found out in each case.

Workers' backgrounds

What is known about these workers' social origins and family histories (their places of origin, castes, religions and languages, relatives' occupations etc.), and how do they see these differences?

Table 13 (p. 26) shows that 73 per cent of workers in the random sample and 64 per cent of the case study sample were born in Mysore State. The next largest group (13, 14 per cent) are from the neighbouring state of Tamil Nadu; the rest come mainly from the other southern states, Andhra and Kerala. Table 14 shows that 44 per cent of the case study sample were brought up in or around Bangalore; 38 per cent are from villages, including villages around Bangalore. (There are no such figures for the random sample.) Many are from regions with a long tradition of emigration, like Kerala or North Arcot District of Tamil Nadu. Most workers who came from distant places already had relatives or close friends working in Bangalore, and stayed with these people until they found permanent jobs – except for skilled men who answered advertisements or were recommended by training institutes, and a minority who came to Bangalore to seek their fortune in a strange city. A few came to stay with relatives in Bangalore as children, to finish their secondary education; others came when their fathers found work in Bangalore and the whole family moved.

It should be clear from the case studies that the common picture of a mass of rootless migrants, 'pushed, not pulled, to the city', and surviving there as marginal men in a hostile urban environment, has no relation to these people (and little relation to most migrants to Bangalore, even casual workers). Migration is sometimes difficult, seldom traumatic. If an immigrant is married, he brings his wife and children with him or soon afterwards; if not, he may marry a girl from his home town or village. He sends regular or occasional gifts of money to his parents, and may bring them to Bangalore when they are old. Distance does not mean a sharp break with family networks and habits: the factory worker's nuclear household acts as the Bangalore end of the family and widens the options open to members elsewhere. Immigrants are not very different from people born in Bangalore.

Nor are there many great differences between people of urban and village origin. Village people, when in Bangalore, do as the Banga-

TABLE 14. *Where workers spent their early childhood (case study sample)*

Bangalore	33%	Villages near Bangalore	11%
Other towns	29	Other villages	27
Total urban	62%	Total rural	38%

NOTE: This is not always the place of birth, because women often give birth at their parents' homes, or in hospital.
The sample for this question was 100 workers.

loreans do without much difficulty: the place itself is largely a collection of urban villages around a modern industrial, commercial and government complex. Though factory workers sometimes discuss specific advantages and disadvantages of town and country life (economic opportunity versus congestion etc.), whether they are of urban or rural origin they do not often talk as if town and country produce different kinds of *people*, with widely differing norms and personalities. Some people have a lasting economic or sentimental interest in land: like Kempayya (p. 114), who thinks of himself as a 'farmer' and may go back to farming when he has saved enough; or the young Brahman communist who says agriculture is 'a free life' and dreams (or just talks?) of dividing the family farm among the labourers and educating them politically (p. 97). These are educated people, from the prosperous rural middle classes, who idealize country life as middle-class townsmen (and sociologists) do. I never heard the same nostalgia for rural life from men whose families were landless labourers or small tenants: they are lucky to have a factory job and they know it. Most immigrants come to town because they believe they can improve their economic situation, and most of them are right.

This last statement, which goes against an anti-urban orthodoxy, lays me open to the objection that workers in the sample factories are the ones who have succeeded largely because they had a headstart: if they are of rural origin, they are drawn largely (not entirely) from prosperous peasant families with access to education, and already 'urbanized' in many ways.

This is partly true; this is not the place to present the (abundant) evidence that many immigrants of humbler rural origins were also right in thinking they could improve their situation, economically and socially, by moving to town. I do not discount the appalling situation of the unemployed and partly employed slum-dwellers: but even this is often better than the situation they have left.

Migration may involve more of a break with country ways in North India. In the south, at least, the typical pattern of migration is from village to small town to city, in one or two generations, or from a village to a nearby city with which the villagers are already familiar. Moreover, South India has a history of migration by families (rather than one man alone) and high urban sex ratios (see p. 11).

More generally, as D. F. Pocock says, 'The sociology of India's urban and rural population may not be divided between urban and rural sociologies'.[1] The 'folk–urban continuum' is really much

---

[1] 'Sociologies: urban and rural', *Contributions to Indian Sociology*, 4 (1960), 63–81 (p. 81).

Life as a factory worker

shorter, and more continuous, than 'urbanization' theory would suggest (following Wirth, Redfield, Hoselitz *et al.*). We are not dealing with two different societies, but with responses to different economic and physical circumstances in a society that is traditionally, profoundly, inextricably urban and rural at the same time: a society divided by great cleavages of interest and consciousness, which cut across the superficial contrast of the 'real India' (rural) and, by implication, the 'false India' of the cities.

'Communities': caste, religion and language

The first categories the people themselves use to distinguish other people's social origins are the traditional ones: caste, and other kinds of 'community'.

Caste, religion and language group are 'communities' in the Indian English sense: ascriptive groups one is born into. ('Communalism' is an excessive attachment to one's own 'community', especially in politics: no one admits to being a communalist.) But people do not divide the social world into 'communities' in a simple unambiguous way, so that a subcaste fits into a caste, which fits into a language group and a religion. 'Community' still counts for a great deal, but only in certain contexts, and the boundaries of the community that count are often shifting and uncertain. Thus a Telugu-speaking Hindu of Naidu caste might identify himself in some situations as a Kannad iga, (i.e. as belonging to the Kannad a-speaking country, in contrast to a Tamil immigrant) and a Yaadava (which can be a Naidu 'subcaste' or an alternative name for the Goll a caste: some Goll as marry some Naidus). He might express agnostic or atheist opinions.

Religion is the most clear-cut 'community', because almost everyone identifies with a religion, conversion is rare and unpopular, and mixed marriage a novelty.[2] Three-quarters of the case study sample are Hindus, a fifth Christians, one a Jain and the rest Muslims.

'Religion' in this sense has little to do with belief (even for Christians and Muslims, who theoretically make faith a test of belonging)

---

[2] Except that some Tamil Harijans ('Untouchables') regard adoption of Hinduism or Christianity as a personal matter, like the traditional Hindu choice of a personal god: so it is quite common to find Harijans and Christians in one Harijan household. There is little missionary work now.

Inter-'caste' marriage is often inter-religious as well, i.e. between Hindus and Christians (seldom Muslims). There are two such marriages in the case study sample, neither involving Harijans.

or with religious practice. Faith makes people take part in devotional cults, or lead certain kinds of lives, or organize their world view in religious terms. Committed communists and some others are actively hostile to 'religion', but there is seldom any doubt about which religious community they come from.[3] A person's religion is his background and culture: it gives him a vocabulary of symbols and associations he can use creatively, to make new statements, if he chooses (e.g. the Hindu idea that time is cyclical and we live on a downslope; with gandhian and other modern variations).

The history of Christianity and Islam in Mysore State is too complex to summarize here. Now Bangalore Muslims tend to be poorly educated, from close-knit urban communities depending on marketplaces and commerce, socially conservative, and dependent for contacts and employment on influential men in their own community. Industrialization has begun to change this, as educated middle-class Muslims have found factory work, and in some cases have moved away from Muslim neighbourhoods. The composition of the random sample suggests that Muslims hold some of the better-paid skilled jobs, especially in public sector factories.

Christians (including Harijan Christians) are on average better educated than their Hindu neighbours, well represented in the professional middle classes, and well placed to find factory work. They are less dependent on each other than Muslims are; more often they are linked to Hindus by ties of culture, economics, neighbourhood, friendship and sometimes kinship.

The Hindu majority are much more diverse. Their consciousness of Hinduism as 'a religion' like Islam or Christianity – rather than a set of castes, with shared sects and cults – may be modern, a reaction to political domination and missionary activity by more self-conscious 'religions' with churches and creeds. But the religious communalism that seems to pervade social and political life in parts of India is the private obsession of small groups here (see pp. 117–18). Even right-wing parties play the religious card discretely, and without much success.

[3] A Muslim trade unionist emphasized that he was descended from Arabs (i.e. from nobility, not from southern Hindus like most local Muslims) and that his grandfather was a noted Urdu poet. His party (the Communist Party of India, CPI), like other parties, makes a special effort to catch the Muslim vote in Muslim areas.

At a Hindu worker's wedding, I asked a full-time union official about the astrological season for weddings. He told me religion was the opiate of the people, and as a communist he was not supposed to know about such things; however. . . . Catholic communists are in a similar case.

In situations where consciousness of communal difference affects or explains behaviour, this is mainly caste consciousness (with the important proviso that someone's assignment to a caste may be uncertain or may depend on the context). The minority religions count almost as castes. Language consciousness cuts across caste boundaries.

Table 15 shows the castes or religions which workers in the case study sample say they belong to. The same degree of detail is not available for the random sample or for Bangalore's population: tables

TABLE 15. *Caste or sect, caste category or religion (case study sample)*

Caste or sect	Number	Block of castes, or religion	Totals	
Brahman (Braahman')	16	Brahman	16	
Mudaliaar	9			
Naidu	6			
Okkaliga	5			
Lingaayat	4			
Deevanga	3			
Nayar	3			
Pill'ai	3	Middle Hindu castes	54	Hindu total 77
Goll'a	2			
Tigal'a	2			
Vishvakarma	2			
Other middle Hindu castes[a]	15			
Aadi Draavid'a (Tamil Harijan)	5	Harijan (Hindu)	7	
Aadi Karnaat'aka (Kannad'a or Telugu Harijan)	2			
Catholic	11			
Protestant	8	Christian	21	
Syrian Christian	2			
Muslim	5	Muslim	5	
Jain (Digaambara)	1	Jain	1	

[a] One of each caste: Aacaari, Arjuna Ks'atra, Cett'i Balija, 'Daivatya Braahman'', Gaund'ar, Karn'ika, Kuncitiga, Kuruba, 'Mahaarast'rian', Naik, Nayak, Redd'i, Washerman; and two men of unidentified caste, probably Okkaligas. Some of these names can be alternative names for castes, or subcaste names (e.g. Cett'i Balija = Naidu).

10 and 11 (p. 25) give figures for each religion and for Scheduled Caste Hindus.

To the extent that a caste *hierarchy* still has practical importance among these Hindu factory workers, it tends to be a ranking of three caste categories: Brahmans, middle castes ('non-Brahmans') and Harijans. In some contexts members of one caste or subcaste may consider themselves more respectable than members of another in the same category: thus some Goll as marry some Naidus but most will not. For most purposes, all castes in the same category are separate but equal. In certain situations, especially in politics, all castes are separate but equal. In some situations (in every situation for a few people), caste does not matter at all.

Consider the different kinds of significance caste can have. It can be a moral structure: traditional caste ideology sees the individual caste as part of a social organism, which is part of a universe in which each part gets value and meaning from its relation to the whole; but the ideological supports of this world view have gone or are going.[4] The caste or 'subcaste' is a group of kin, a field in which to find marriage partners for one's children and to make useful alliances by marriage (see pp. 79–81). The caste is a wider network of contacts, which can be exploited to find jobs or get things done: any vestige of moral obligation, or reciprocity, or patron–client relations, is worth trying in a situation of uncertainty and cut-throat competition. Caste can be simply an explanation of things: some people really do get jobs or promotion because of their caste, or partly because of it. In most cases it is a false explanation, as it is for 'communalists' who blame every failure on belonging to the wrong caste: this is what a marxist would call 'false consciousness' of their class position. Caste can and always could be a code for economic class differences: traditional caste hierarchies could accommodate changes in the wealth and power of castes, or *ad hoc* splinter subcastes, and caste ideology provided logically strong explanations to reconcile visible social mobility with the eternal caste order.[5] The argument about whether class is 'replacing' caste rests on a confusion between the people's own categories and outsiders' comparative categories, except to the extent

[4] This is not something obvious or inevitable in an industrializing society, but it is happening all the same. It needs to be shown, not assumed: see some of the career histories in ch. 4, and Holmström, 'Caste and status in an Indian city'.

[5] See M. N. Srinivas, *Caste in modern India* (Bombay, 1962); J. Silverberg (ed.), *Social mobility in the caste system in India* (The Hague, 1968); D. F. Pocock, *Kanbi and Patidar* (Oxford, 1972); and Pocock, 'The movement of castes', *Man*, 55 (May 1955), 71–2.

that indigenous concepts are emerging, more like western uses of 'class' and *seen* as alternatives to 'caste'.[6]

Caste could accommodate, and explain away, more social mobility than is often supposed. But there is a limit: the great variety of new occupations, together with partly independent ideological changes, make caste more and more unreliable as a coding of class differences, though still a useful sign of people's social origins. Thus many 'middle'-caste workers come from traditionally dominant castes of farmers or traders: Okkaligas from Mysore, Mudaliaars from Tamil Nadu, Naidus from Andhra. The Aadi Draavid'as ('original Dravidians', the modern name for Tamil-speaking Harijans) are immigrants, less bound to traditional labouring and menial work than the Kannad'a- or Telugu-speaking local Harijans, or Aadi Karnaat'akas. Among Christians, immigrants from Kerala tend to be well educated, ambitious and successful: especially the Syrian Christians, the ancient church of Kerala, who behave as a high caste.

High-caste Hindus, mainly Brahmans, are strongly represented in managerial and skilled jobs, especially in one factory. But Brahmans do almost anything – technical, clerical, and even unskilled casual jobs which they take in the hope of moving on to something else. They tend to be sons of clerks, lower government officials, small businessmen or village landlords.

Middle-caste Hindus, found in most jobs except cleaning, are often sons of owner or tenant farmers, craftsmen, shopkeepers, petty officials or owners of small businesses.

Many menial and unskilled workers, especially cleaners and watchmen, are Harijans. Educated Harijans are quite well represented in skilled and semi-skilled jobs: public sector factories must take a Harijan quota, and private ones are under some official pressure to do so. Several Harijan workers said their fathers and grandfathers were in the army or police: this confirmed my strong impression, from earlier fieldwork, that these have been the chief paths of upward mobility for Harijans in the past, and that the present generation of Harijans able to take advantage of government educational concessions and job reservation come from an army or police background.

Tables 16 and 17 summarize the information I have on the occupations of workers' fathers and grandfathers. I have not analysed the life histories of informants' siblings and other relatives, though the material is in my field notes.

Just as 'religion', as a way of grouping people, has little to do with

[6] See Béteille's comments on Bengali terms for 'class' in footnote 2, p. 123.

'Communities': caste, religion and language

TABLE 16. *Father's occupation and caste category or religion (case study sample)*

Father's occupation	Brahmans (%)	Middle Hindu castes (%)	Harijans (%)	Christians (%)	Muslims (%)	Total (%)
Farmer, farm labourer, fisherman etc. (including village landlord)[a]	3	14	2	5	1	25
Unskilled manual worker (not agricultural)	–	1	1	–	–	2
Skilled manual worker, craftsman	1	10	1	2	–	14
Clerical, office or sales worker, or lower government official	5	9	–	5	1	20
Teacher	2	3	–	1	–	6
Owner of a small business	3	9	–	3	1	16
Professional, higher government official, graduate technician etc.	1	1	–	–	1	3
Armed forces or police	–	3	3	3	1	10
Not known	2	–	–	1	–	3
Total	17	50	7	20	5	99

[a] This covers everyone in agriculture. Indian land tenures are complicated, and with the information given it was impossible to distinguish consistently between big and small landowners, tenants, sharecroppers and landless labourers.

Compare 'Analysis of backgrounds of candidates applying for industrial employment, 1963', (by skill, community, education, parents' occupation etc.), using figures supplied by Simpson's Industrial Health Service, Madras, in M. Singer, *When a great tradition modernizes* (New York, 1972), pp. 374f.

worship or faith, or 'caste' with traditional occupations and religious purity, so 'language' has not much to do with communication. Most people speak two or three languages anyway. One's mother tongue is a sign of other differences and claims.

First it is a sign of where one comes from, or is thought to belong. Since states were reorganized on linguistic lines, each southern state is the area where a majority speak one of the four main Dravidian languages. Bangalore is odd, because it is the capital of the Kannada-speaking state, yet since the last century Tamils have been the biggest

35

TABLE 17. *Paternal grandfather's occupation and caste category or religion (case study sample)*

Paternal grandfather's occupation	Brahmans (%)	Middle Hindu castes (%)	Harijans (%)	Christians (%)	Muslims (%)	Total (%)
Farmer, farm labourer, fisherman etc. (including village landlord)	7	22	3	10	2	44
Unskilled manual worker (not agricultural)	–	1	–	–	–	1
Skilled manual worker, craftsman	1	7	–	–	–	8
Clerical, office or sales worker, or lower government official	2	3	–	–	–	5
Teacher	1	–	–	–	1	2
Owner of a small business	–	8	–	–	–	8
Professional, higher government official, graduate technician etc.	1	–	–	–	–	1
Armed forces or police	–	2	3	1	1	7
Other known occupation	2	–	–	1	–	3
Not known	3	7	1	8	1	20
Total	17	50	7	20	5	99

single language group in the city: no group has a majority. Kannad'a immigration is probably tipping the balance now.[7]

Many Kannad'igas (Kannad'a speakers) see themselves as 'sons of the soil', with a moral claim to jobs taken from them by clever immigrants, especially Tamils, and Malayalis. The Kannad'a communalist parties, and Kannad'a cultural organizations and public figures, demand privileges for Mysore people or for Kannad'igas. In public (to journalists, or to me) they sometimes say this means Mysore-born people, or those who learn Kannad'a. This need not be taken seriously: language is a community of birth.[8]

---

[7] Tables 12 and 13 (pp. 25 and 26) show the languages and states of birth of the random sample and case study sample.

[8] Some castes have another first language but align themselves with Kannad'igas against 'immigrants' (e.g. Telugu-speaking castes long settled in Mysore, in-

'Communities': caste, religion and language

In chapter 4 (pp. 117–18) I describe the 'communalist' attitude of those who believe their own careers are blocked, because other 'communities' have all the right contacts and promote their own men. Many more people make remarks that show the same kind of prejudice (a factory officer: These Tamils are very clever, and once they get a factory job they try to bring in all their friends and relatives; Tamil workers: Kannad́a is an undeveloped language, the Kannad́igas have no ancient culture as we have, they are all peasants so naturally they don't take to factory work as we do; Kannad́igas: 'These dirty Tamils'; and so on). Some turn to violence: at the gates of one public sector factory, gangs of unemployed Kannad́igas demanding jobs, organized by the Kannad́a–communalist parties, held repeated demonstrations for several weeks, and some workers were injured. Minor quarrels led to fights inside the factory, until the management sacked a handful of workers and the police acted firmly against the demonstrators outside. In two other factories in my sample, a slate of candidates composed largely of one language group were accused by their opponents of using language loyalties to get elected, and of helping only their own people with promotions and grievances.

Yet the real 'communalists' – obsessed with the obstacles put in their way by other communities – are a minority among factory workers. 'Communalism' is an explanation of failure, but getting a factory job is already a success.

Subsequent disappointments, unlike the agonizing failure to get any decent job at all, are less easily covered by the 'communalist' explanation. It was the unemployed demonstrators outside the factory gate who caused serious injuries: the fights in the factory were trivial. Those factory workers who grumble occasionally about the way other communities are getting ahead regard 'communalist' agitation as the work of demagogues and loafers with nothing better to do: it is the contempt of the middle class for the rabble.

On the city scale, language consciousness is partly a code for class consciousness (a marxist would say: 'false consciousness'). Groups have unequal access to secondary and technical education, useful contacts and organized sector jobs. 'Communalism' (in language, caste or religion) explains why some have advantages.

cluding landowning castes in some villages around Bangalore, and most local non-Tamil Harijans). A farming caste of the region (Tigaĺas) speak a Tamil dialect but distinguish themselves from Tamil immigrants.

On the problem of reconciling national unity, and the need for qualified labour, with demands for special treatment of 'sons of the soil' in other states, see *Report of the National Commission on Labour*, pp. 64, 74.

Life as a factory worker

But if language consciousness is a distorted form of class consciousness, it is also a claim to solidarity across caste lines: each language group has its high, middle and low castes. Even the humblest citizen, if he belongs to the *land*, has a claim to some privileges there: and everyone belongs to some land. So the language 'communalist' is an equalitarian of a kind. He has a mental map of society divided into castes, but castes grouped in a new way – not in a hierarchy, but in virtue of an association with the land which is shared equally by all indigenous castes.[9]

Education and training

Tables 8 and 9 (pp. 23, 24) show that half the workers in the random sample have a Senior School Leaving Certificate (SSLC); three-quarters reached high school; and a quarter have some formal technical qualification. Clearly most of them come from minorities with access to secondary education: either the middle class (including well-off peasant families), who send their sons and daughters to high school as a matter of course, or people from areas like Kerala and Bangalore itself, where primary education is almost universal and a large proportion go on to high school; or Harijans who get government scholarships and places in school hostels.

Increasingly, SSLC is required for any factory work except a few menial jobs: it is more important than any technical qualification taken before the worker gets his first job. SSLC shows that the applicant has some general knowledge of mathematics, and especially English, which is generally used for training and for giving instructions. 'SSLC Failed' is sometimes enough: it shows that the student stayed the course until the examination, which is something of a lottery anyway; and a student who failed SSLC is eligible for an Industrial Training Institute (ITI) course. As competition for jobs becomes more intense, educational standards among factory workers are rising fast – probably faster than in the general population.

Table 18 shows that the proportion with technical qualifications does not vary much with age: this is partly because these can be acquired in the course of a career (at work or evening classes), and because managements sometimes doubt the value of paper qualifications as against experience, except in specialized trades like tool and die making. Sometimes managements do not want experience. The

[9] On caste, language politics and class consciousness in a rather similar situation, see H. C. Hart, 'Urban politics in Bombay: the meaning of community', *Economic Weekly*, special number, June 1960, 983–8.

Education and training

TABLE 18. *Age, general education and formal technical qualifications (random sample, men)*

Age	With SSLC or better (%)	With formal technical qualification (%)
Up to 25	72	24
25–9	59	26
30–4	50	29
35–9	45	24
40–4	42	28
45–9	33	19
50 and over	29	21
All ages	52	26

NOTE: Women's situation is different; and the sample of women is too small.

personnel manager of a private firm said they prefer to train young men fresh from school for semi-skilled jobs ('Their future is in this company, they feel that their bread is here') rather than men who are used to a different style of work in another factory or workshop. For skilled jobs, they prefer men fresh from training institutes, with a diploma or certificate.

What are the real chances and choices in education facing factory workers or their parents (or workers now planning their children's education)?

For these families, there are few choices. Parents say children should get as much education as they can, and the rest depends on luck. Only a few say their children should not be educated beyond a certain point (one man said his sons should have just enough education to read blueprints and do toolroom work, like himself: too many double graduates are unemployed). Many more say their children should try to get higher education, to be doctors, engineers etc.: this is largely dreaming, or what one says to an outsider who asks. In practice the goal is usually SSLC at least – it is a necessary condition for a good job, though no longer a sufficient one. It is quite common to study for another year or two until one drops out, because of examination failure ('ill health') or expense.

The schools available are mostly municipal or government schools using regional languages, but teaching English as well. Classes are large, schools are badly equipped, teachers are harrassed and not well paid; so students who do not come from an educated home find it hard to keep up. Many Bangalore children from this kind of background

39

go to evening classes as well, ranging from tutorials given by regular teachers earning extra money, and free classes put on by religious or charitable organizations (sometimes by educated factory workers), to 'homework classes' where children sit in a crowded and badly lit room, under the eye of a woman who keeps them quiet and gives minimal help with their homework. A few workers went to English-medium schools, often mission schools.

SSLC, taken around the age of 16, covers science and arts subjects. Specialization begins later: most students (or their parents) choose technical subjects, science or commerce. Six per cent of the random sample are graduates, often but not always in office jobs (the sample of 'workers' includes lower management staff in one factory). Another 7 per cent passed the Intermediate or Pre-University examinations, and many of these began a degree course. These days a graduate is lucky to get a factory job: some wait for years.

After SSLC, some young men go straight into a job (usually but not always on someone's recommendation: see 'Finding a job', pp. 42ff.), and receive perhaps six months' training in the training section or on the job. Some go for technical training, either as apprentices, or at government Industrial Training Institutes, polytechnics etc. The others are unemployed, or take casual work as 'helpers' in small workshops or provision shops – often for years – while they look for steady jobs.

Under the Apprentices Act (1961) all industrial concerns must train a number of apprentices, in proportion to their total work force; but they are not required to employ the apprentices afterwards. Apprenticeships generally last from two to four years. Firms with vacancies will often give preference to promising apprentices who know the ways of the firm: so although ex-apprentices may have to wait six months before going back to the same factory, many do so in the end. And a man who has satisfactorily completed an apprenticeship at a good factory has a good chance of finding a job soon. One Bangalore factory making car components (not in the sample) advertises 20 apprenticeships every six months, and expects 8 000 applications. Only men with an excellent general education have a chance, even if personal influence helps.

A much larger number (7 per cent of the random sample) go to an Industrial Training Institute after passing or failing SSLC. Selection is by interview and tests of general knowledge or aptitude: I do not think influence counts for much, because no one alleges that it does. Trainees get a stipend. The course lasts eighteen months, or two years with in-plant training, and leads to a certificate which is useful in job-seeking, though no guarantee of a job. Personnel managers sometimes ring up the local ITI and ask for recruits.[10]

Various government and private institutes and polytechnics (including a polytechnic attached to one private electrical factory) train students for higher qualifications, like the diploma or licentiate in engineering. Eight per cent of the random sample have these or comparable diplomas, which take at least three years. Another 9 per cent have certificates of some kind (e.g. in typing). Some firms provide technical evening classes, release workers for classes outside, or send them away for advanced training – in some cases, to Germany, so that ambitious married workers face a hard decision, whether to be separated from their families for three years or more.

Paper qualifications are especially important for young men entering the work force, as competition becomes fiercer and managements demand higher qualifications. For these young men and their families, there is no gradual progress through a number of stages and successive opportunities: each obstacle overcome – SSLC, Intermediate, ITI certificate, apprenticeship or temporary job – slightly increases the chances of winning the one big prize, which is *permanent* employment, a place in the citadel. Once inside the citadel, with a job to fall back on, improving one's qualifications and getting promotion becomes a gradual process, a matter of more or less, faster or slower progress, rather than simply of having a permanent job or not having one.

Because of rising standards, older workers who were recruited when it was easy to get a job now find it hard to get promotion except by seniority, and hard to change jobs. Most lack the necessary basic education, time or energy for evening classes, or the luck or influence to be chosen for an apprenticeship or special course. These men feel unjustly treated. They say their experience is worth more than a paper qualification and should be recognized; they dwell on young workers' incompetence, and they list all the techniques they themselves have learned without getting any qualifications. And they may

---

[10] In a useful account of apprenticeship schemes and of the 337 ITIs, A. de Souza says the ITIs are badly equipped; students are told how to use tools but have few opportunities to use them; and curricula are over-specialized in particular trades so that ITI graduates are 'usually unprepared for immediate employment in industry'. He argues for more versatile vocational education, imparting knowledge and skills basic to a number of related trades ('Education for employment' in Fonseca (ed.), *Challenge of poverty in India*, pp. 128–45). But firms in my sample are quite willing to take ITI graduates for further training in their own training sections, or on the job. The situation may be different in smaller firms, or those without well-equipped training sections.

often be right, since a young man will often go for a paper qualification – any qualification, at any sort of training institute – simply to
make his name stand out on the long lists of applicants. Thus one
man with ten years' experience of a specialized production process
was awaiting the result of an application for another job: what worried
him was that he had no paper qualification, though he had heard
somewhere that the government planned to recognize ten years'
experience of skilled work as equivalent to a diploma in engineering,
and he wanted to know if this was true.

Will this year's recruits be in the same situation ten years from
now?

Finding a job

The big step is the one that gets you into the citadel of permanent
employment in a modern, organized sector industry. Once in, you
expect to stay (though not necessarily with the same firm) and
usually do stay. Table 19 shows how the case study sample say they
got their present job (which, for 42 per cent, is also their first job).
I have no such figures for the random sample, except those given
in table 20. These tables do not distinguish between those who went
straight into a permanent job, and those who were first taken on as
temporary workers. A few made contacts inside the factory while
working for building contractors on the site.

The biggest single group say they answered newspaper advertisements (the proportion would probably be less for the whole work
force). These are often placed in English-language papers only. Young
men looking for jobs spend much of their time in municipal or
charitable 'reading rooms' in Bangalore, not only to scan the papers
for jobs but to pass the time and meet friends.

Most men who answered advertisements, and some who applied
independently, say they used no personal influence or recommendation. Can this be true? Undoubtedly some make it a point of pride that
they got jobs and promotion on merit; some want to show that merit
(which got them their jobs, but not promotion) goes unrewarded;
some would have used influential friends if they had had any; and
some gave me the answer they thought I would approve of.

While 44 per cent of the whole sample (recruited by methods i–ii)
say they did not use influential friends, another 32 per cent (methods
iii–iv) say plainly that they did. Of course some kinds of influence are
more effective than others. One factory owner recruits some young
men directly from his home town (see 'Factory owner's kith and

Finding a job

TABLE 19. *Method of recruitment (case study sample)*

	Public sector (%)	Private sector (%)	Whole sample (%)
(i) Answered newspaper advertisement: no personal recommendation (according to informant)	45	27	36
(ii) Applied independently to factory: no personal recommendation	4	11	8
(iii) Applied through a factory officer	2	9	6
(iv) Applied through a relative working in the factory	8	5	7
(v) Applied through another worker in the factory	4	9	7
(vi) Applied through an influential outsider (e.g. politician, official, businessman)	4	11	8
(vii) Factory owner's kith and kin (12% in one factory only)	0	7	4
(viii) Factory recruited directly (e.g. from Industrial Training Institutes)	6	2	4
(ix) Recruited to play in factory football team	4	0	2
(x) Other methods, or not known	22	18	20

NOTE: The sample of 104 workers included 49 in the public sector, 55 in the private.

TABLE 20. *Was a relative already in the factory when this worker applied? (random sample)*

	Public sector (%)	Private sector (%)	Whole sample (%)
Yes	6	8	7
No	35	79	50
Not known	59	14	43

SOURCE: Information available in factory files on the sample of 1134 workers (65 per cent in the public sector, 35 per cent in the private).

43

kin', pp. 106–8). Some factory officers or foreign technicians are in a position to promise a job to someone recommended to them, or to a servant's son. A politician, or a business connexion of the management, may be able to promise a job with the same confidence. But the inside contact is usually a foreman, or an applicant's friend or relative, who puts in a word for the applicant and gets him an interview. Workers and managements say influence can get someone an interview, but only merit can get him through it: thus one foreman said a young man was interviewed because he was his cousin but appointed entirely on aptitude and qualifications. 'Merit' is ambiguous; but managements have an interest in appointing men whose relatives or friends will vouch for them (and in putting employees under an obligation), while keeping incompetent workers out.

This pattern of recruitment (contacts + 'merit') applies especially in the private sector, where these things can be arranged more directly. When the queue of apparently qualified applicants is long, the rational personnel officer – who cannot interview them all but wants a contented work force – sees the man with the right contacts first. The same thing applies, though much less, to the more diffuse kinds of influence which come from belonging to the right caste or language group: why not choose the people whose ways you know, keep the right balance in the factory, and everyone as happy as possible? It is not always a matter of some deep, primordial loyalty.

The applicant generally writes a letter, and then fills in a form. These go into his file. The letters are usually typed in stilted English by a job typist, who puts in a little information given by the applicant (e.g. that he is skilled, or Scheduled Caste) and sometimes a conventional plea to help him because he is his parents' or siblings' only support. The form asks for education and experience, father's occupation, religion, languages, health, salary expected, relatives or friends in the company, two 'responsible' referees, whether the applicant is a deserter or has a criminal record and so on. At the interview, company officers ask him about his schooling, his work record, if any, his family, plans for the future, spare-time interests and general knowledge (like the names of ministers, or distances). For skilled trades there may be an aptitude test. Last of all, there is a medical examination. If the applicant clears all these hurdles, he may have to wait for some weeks or months before starting work, or even getting an offer. Meanwhile he needs somewhere to live, and something to live on: i.e. relatives, if possible.

Half the random sample had a job before their present one; and half were in their present job by the age of 23 (see tables 21 and 22). The case study sample are a little younger and appear to have had more previous jobs, but this may be because I recorded a wider range of previous jobs in workers' life histories (including many jobs in the unorganized sector) than the ones listed in application forms. Skilled

TABLE 21. *Number of previous jobs (both samples, men)*

Previous jobs	Random sample (%)	Case study sample (%)
None	50	42
1	33	26
2	10	11
3	5	10
4	2	5
5 or more	1	6
Median	1 job	1 job
Mean (taking '5 or more' as 5)	0.8	1.3

NOTE: Though some managers told me that labour turnover was, or was not, a problem for them, I was not able to get any figures for turnover in particular factories (see 'Changing jobs', p. 57).

TABLE 22. *Age at appointment to present job (both samples, men), and mean number of previous jobs (random sample only, men)*

Age at appointment	Percentage of case study sample	Percentage of random sample	Mean number previous jobs (random sample)
15–19	40[a]	13	0.2
20–4	41	51	0.5
25–9	13	23	1.2
30–4	1	8	1.5
35–9	4	3	1.5
40+	1	1	2.5
Median age of sample	29	31	
Median age at appointment	20	23	
Mean age at appointment	22	24	

[a] But more than half of these were appointed at 19.

or semi-skilled men will list jobs in other factories, in garages where they have learned a mechanical skill; but years spent serving in a retail shop, or in a marginal workshop with primitive equipment, are not qualifications one wants to advertise.

For a young man who does not go straight from school or training institute into the organized sector (sometimes with a period of waiting at home) the options close early: there is not much chance for a man who is outside the citadel at 25, unless he has a special skill. The best thing is to stay in Bangalore, acquire skills and contacts wherever you can, read the papers and hope for luck. Once in the citadel, there may be opportunities to change jobs later.

Recruitment is 'lumpy'. Turnover is low, promotion slow, and these factories are not yet losing many men through retirement. The supply of new permanent jobs fluctuates widely because of booms and recessions in the national economy (e.g. the 1964–5 recession, followed by a boom around 1970) and decisions to locate new developments in Bangalore, made by the government or by industrialists (Bengali businessmen fleeing from 'red' Calcutta, Asians forced out of East Africa). Most new jobs are in new factories or major expansion projects, involving a single massive raid on the labour market. This affects new entrants directly or indirectly (by depleting the skilled work force in other factories), but in both cases suddenly. If you miss your chance around the age of 20 you may never get another.

What recruiting policies do managements follow? To the extent that there is a consistent policy in a firm, this is a working compromise between publicly declared policies (in union agreements, government directives etc.), union and political pressures, past practice, different officers' ideas about what ought to be done, and pressures on the man formally responsible for recruitment (usually the personnel officer).

In reporting the following conversations with personnel officers, I make no distinction between public and private sectors, or between the sample and some other Bangalore factories, to protect the officers' anonymity.

Personnel officer 1: his firm is expanding. They recruit skilled workers by advertisement or through training institutes, others by casual application. All applicants must have SSLC, or 'Failed SSLC' for an unskilled job. Except for highly skilled men, they take only young men under 25 without experience who can get used to the ways of this factory. Young men fresh from school or training institute can be trained in the factory: 'Their future is in this company, they feel that their bread is here.' And the firm prefers local candidates, who are less likely to leave and will be 'satisfied with whatever we give'. (In fact, this firm pays very well.) Young men with SSLC are often taken on as temporary workers for a year, to make sure they are suitable.

The criteria for appointment are (1) local candidate, (2) physically fit, (3) qualification (general education; or, for highly skilled men like tool-makers, experience, a four-year apprenticeship, or a specialized course at certain institutes), (4) background (the family should live in Bangalore, preferably near the factory in a permanent house; the applicant's father and brothers should be educated and well placed in life – 'that shows the sons will not go astray' – and he should have references from known persons). No preference is given to employees' relatives. (This is not true.) In some cases the candidate gets aptitude test as well: in maths, general knowledge, and handling the factory's products. Highly skilled workers are tested more thoroughly, and interviewed by a panel including a Director.

Personnel officer 2: his firm has reached 'saturation point', and hardly recruits anyone except replacements. Applicants (except the few labourers and sweepers) must have reached Standard IX, effectively SSLC because of the competition. Most are local people, but they get no preference; many come through the Employment Exchange (this is the only firm where I met anyone who got his job this way). The firm is under political pressure to take Kannad'a speakers. They give preference to employees' relatives, especially on compassionate grounds when a breadwinner dies. (One man had to wait six months after his father died, but was not worried because he knew the firm must give him a job in the end. This firm even runs an ancillary workshop, employing workers' widows and other women relatives; so a job here is almost heritable property.) The firm tries to train its own skilled men, and to fill skilled jobs by internal recruitment.

Personnel officer 3: his firm recruits only replacements, but in large num-bers because high turnover of workers is their main problem. (This is unusual.) They generally advertise vacancies, and recruit 'people with just the required qualification – neither above nor below'. For skilled jobs, they take men who have spent eighteen months at an Industrial Training Institute: not unemployed graduate engineers who get discontented and expect more because they are graduates – 'then ultimately you get the love letter, as they say, from the union'. Unskilled workers do not need much intelligence or education 'as long as they are hefty'. (Another personnel officer will not take applicants with SSLC for unskilled jobs, because this creates 'problems'.) After four or five years' work an unskilled worker will come crying, saying he wants to marry but no one will take him because he is only a labourer; so the firm may give him semi-skilled work. When someone leaves, the firm asks: was his job necessary? When you recruit a man it means costs – you are taking him on 'for all time to come' (i.e. until *he* chooses to leave); 'and it isn't fair to recruit today and retrench tomorrow, because it affects the morale of the industry' (i.e. the union will make trouble).

Personnel officer 4: his firm employs mainly semi-skilled workers, and many women. The original work force was recruited through office contacts, the police etc. Now the firm is expanding, and puts more emphasis on education. No one without SSLC has been recruited for the last two years. The firm prefers school-leavers who can be trained in the firm's excellent training section or on the job. It seldom uses the Employment Exchange, which cannot supply skilled men when they are needed.

The policy is to take at least one relative of each employee (often wives, or girls who have sat at home sewing since leaving school), sometimes more – but not too many. Inefficient workers are not promoted but seldom sacked.

Workers say: the firm recruits some skilled men directly from an institute in another state (without regard to caste). This is a good firm to work for, but the Managing Director's caste get preference.

Proposals for agreement with a union: vacancies at the lowest grade shall be filled by external recruitment, with priority for deceased employees' relations, ex-servicemen, and employees retrenched by similar undertakings elsewhere. Qualified candidates shall be interviewed and marked, but the quota for Scheduled Caste employees shall be followed strictly, whether they get enough marks or not. Intermediate grades shall be filled by promotion if possible; some technical grades, 70 per cent by direct recruitment, the rest by promotion; the highest grade below management by promotion on 'merit' only, not seniority. 'The decision to fill up or not to fill up vacancies shall rest with the management.'

From the firms' point of view, previous experience is valuable for skilled men, not others, and sometimes a disadvantage (the applicant may have learned different work habits, expect too much, and lack commitment to the firm). For most (semi-skilled) jobs, the ideal applicant is young, with SSLC, and from a middle-class family living locally. An Industrial Training Institute diploma is useful, not essential.

Such men are easy to find: by advertising; by asking factory officers, business contacts, or principals of training institutes; or by passing the word around and awaiting applications. Few firms find the Employment Exchange helpful.

All firms give preference to employees' relatives (not only on compassionate grounds), whether they admit it or not. Some try to impose a quota, e.g. one relative per employee. All take *qualified* applicants, at least, when recommended by a factory officer, or an official or business contact, but generally do not admit it.

Public sector recruitment is more formal and bureaucratic, and 'fairer', giving more weight to paper qualifications and social considerations (especially the Scheduled Caste quota).

What do workers think generally happens (as distinct from what happened to them personally) and what do they think ought to happen?

There are four ways to get a job: luck, unfair influence, justified use of personal connexions or status, and 'merit'.

In a competitive market, it is hard to blame anyone for using almost any advantage to get a job: for who shall cast the first stone? (One moralistic young man: 'If the only way is muddy, you must pass along it.') But the system is not considered fair; nor are particular managements, in giving so much weight to influence.

If one asks: 'How do most people get their jobs?', the commonest answer is: by influence, knowing the management or a friend of the management or someone who can put pressure on the management, by bribery, or by belonging to the right caste. For obvious reasons, unorganized sector workers and the unemployed say the same, with more conviction and bitterness.

No one admits he got his job through bribery. I doubt whether anyone bribable is in a position to guarantee a job in the sample factories, except possibly in one. It may or may not be possible to buy a job in some older factories: in one it is alleged that the union can sell a job for Rs 2500. But many workers (as the case studies show) got their jobs through an influential man: a politician, an uncle working in a government office which controls supplies, an engineer who knew the Managing Director.

By implication, all these methods are unfair, at least when used by someone else. Fair means are 'merit' (ambiguous, but implying some element of achievement) or being a deserving case: a dead employee's son or widow who deserves a job on 'compassionate' grounds, a 'political sufferer' for Independence or ex-serviceman, a Kannad´iga who deserves priority as a 'son of the soil', or a Harijan (because Gandhi said, and the Indian Constitution recognizes, that the injustice done to 'Untouchables' must be righted).

Relatives of a dead employee deserve jobs: but what about those of a living employee? The men I knew are now in a position to bring in their younger brothers or more distant relatives, and morally obliged to do so if they can. What about the whole educated lower-middle class from which they come? Are not these people fitted for jobs by their education, their background, their sense of responsibility? Are they not *entitled* to jobs? After all (the argument goes), the middle classes are at a disadvantage because they cannot take up just any job, as a labourer can. This is what I call the 'divine right of the middle classes'; but most workers will not push the argument so far.[11]

Some men say proudly that they got their jobs entirely on merit, without recommendations or influence. If they had previous jobs, 'merit' means skill and experience (as it does for promotion). But it cannot mean this for those taking a first job, except to the extent that a training institute qualification is evidence of skill. Here 'merit' means aptitude or potential demonstrated by success in education, interviews and tests. Getting a job by merit means little more than *not* getting it by influence or luck.

In the end, a great deal depends on sheer luck: other people's jobs, and one's own.

Merit is opposed to luck (including influence). Is it a moral and/or innate quality? Is it some general quality one has or lacks, or does it consist of the qualities practically required for the job? (The more it depends on contingencies of the job market – the skills that happen to be in demand – the less it can be seen as a moral quality.) The closest analogy I can think of is 'intelligence' in England: a quasi-moral quality, which can be measured 'scientifically' (as IQ) but which gives a justified moral claim to education and a good job. In both cases, the ideology is one of achievement: achieved status is *morally* better than ascribed status or luck.[12] So a Brahman clerk claimed he got all his jobs by merit except, unfortunately, one, which he got through his uncle. An educated Harijan, who said he had got his job without recommendations, was acutely embarrassed when his brother suggested a relative had also helped, and denied it. The less skilled, less educated or more realistic workers know that 'merit' may be better, but luck counts for most.

This ideology of merit is a way of moralizing the labour market, and it involves a conscious rejection of the dominant traditional justification for inequality: caste. I argue below (pp. 140–2) that this devaluing of caste is not simply the result of importing foreign ideas, but the continuation of an old anticaste tradition in new circumstances.

[11] This use of 'middle class' may seem surprising. These factory workers call themselves 'working class' or 'middle class'; and this Indian use of 'middle class' reflects the real situation well (see pp. 137–8).

[12] This is why working-class origins are such a plus in middle-class England now: the successful man who has raised himself from working-class origins proves that merit is really rewarded, and shows other middle-class people that they have it, too. The position of the working-class person who *stays* in the working class is different.

J. N. Sinha notes that census and official figures show more unemployment in relatively prosperous states of India:[13]

> This clearly means that those who are poor cannot afford to remain unemployed ... The unemployment we know of is the unemployment of those who have the means to maintain themselves during the period of unemployment. So though it may appear a bit strange, I would hold that unemployment is in the nature of a luxury which only the well-to-do can afford.

The educated wait for the right job, with promotion prospects, so 'the period of unemployment for them is really similar to that of investment, which brings a higher rate of return in the form of higher lifetime earnings' (p. 160).

This applies to some of the workers described here – especially those who got their first, and present, job around the age of 20. Their families (parents or brothers, or more distant relatives living in Bangalore) or friends gave them a place to live and fed them while they looked or simply waited for a job. Some worried; some did not, but spent their time quite happily talking to friends, reading, playing football and so on. Some had no need to worry.

But unemployment is not a middle-class luxury for the men who move from job to job, to gain experience and maintain themselves while looking for something better. This is why young men will take casual work as 'helpers' at Rs 40 (approximately £2) a month, in badly equipped small workshops. Without experience it is hard to get any job, and without a job one will never get experience.[14] The solution is to wait for a lucky break – a casual job, preferably in the organized sector, which then becomes 'temporary' or even permanent.[15]

---

[13] 'Poverty and unemployment' in Fonseca (ed.), *Challenge of poverty in India*, pp. 159–65 (p. 159). 'Unemployment' is notoriously hard to define, but comparisons between state unemployment rates within India are probably significant.

[14] The *Report of the National Commission on Labour* discusses this vicious circle, and suggests more stipendiary apprenticeships.

[15] Or to fake experience – to take a permanent job on the strength of non-existent experience and hope the office will never find out. One young man, whom I knew in my previous fieldwork, got a good job by claiming he had worked for some years in a garage: he promised to bring testimonials. Some time later the office reminded him of this. He put them off for a year, saying the partners running the garage had split up, one had died and so on. The office appeared to forget about the matter. Meanwhile he acquired genuine experience in the factory and moved to a better job in another.

Life as a factory worker

A career in the factory

Once inside the citadel, a man's real career begins, because he has security and can plan ahead. The big jump is from not having an organized sector job to having one. After that the career is a more continuous graduated movement; and almost always *upwards*, whether fast or slow.

Of course the security is not absolute: Employees' State Insurance and relatives are a frail protection against permanent illness or the closing of a factory, and the dangers are slightly greater in the private sector. They can be reduced by a strategy of safety first, never moving forwards without a secure position to fall back on.

'Career' in this context means movement up the ladder of income, also the things which usually go with higher income – independence, command, respect, more interesting work, better chances of moving, still more security ... One man's upward movement improves the chances for his children, and his wife if she wants a job, and often other kin as well.

A worker is recruited (often after a spell as a temporary or casual worker or an apprentice) to a particular job (e.g. press operator), which belongs to a grade or category. Most factories have about seven grades below 'officers', and each grade is described as unskilled, semi-skilled, skilled or sometimes highly skilled.

Each grade has about twelve steps. A worker is usually appointed to the lowest step in his grade, and moves up one step every year. His grade and step determine his basic salary: other payments (Dearness Allowance, annual and incentive bonuses, overtime etc.) partly depend on his basic salary.

Some workers say 'promotion' for them means yearly increments: they expect nothing more. But there are also double increments, semi-automatic promotion to a higher grade when a man reaches the top of his grade, and promotion on merit. Promotion to a higher grade may involve a new kind of work, or higher pay for doing the same work with a new title. It is hard but possible for a worker to become an 'officer'.

So the ways for a worker to raise his income are: (1) yearly increments, with semi-automatic promotion after a number of years (the slowest way, but sure); (2) real promotion; (3) moonlighting (doing another job in the evenings and at weekends); and (4) changing jobs (including the maximum-risk strategy, which is to start one's own business).

A career in the factory

The model for the factory hierarchy is British rather than Japanese. Ranks are not distinguished from functions, and in principle 'a man is paid for what he *does* (actually or fictionally) not for what he *can* do'.[16] But seniority counts for more than in the older British model, even if long service has to be rationalized as experience and acquired skill, and job classifications must be made to fit. These organized sector firms have the features which, Dore says, show that British firms too are moving in the Japanese direction (p. 352):

1. increasing welfare and security benefits.
2. increasing recognition of seniority.
3. changes in the status system, particularly an erosion of the manual/white-collar divide.

In the Indian factory hierarchy, there are fairly clear but not watertight boundaries between these broad categories (excluding trainees and apprentices):

top management and owners;
officers (middle management);
skilled workers (and sometimes another 'highly skilled' category);
semi-skilled workers;
permanent unskilled workers;
casual or temporary workers.

A man has a chance of rising from one broad category into the one above, but generally no higher, unless he moves to another firm – except for educated casual or temporary workers who go straight into a semi-skilled or skilled job when there is a vacancy.

It is possible to see this factory hierarchy as a modern equivalent of the traditional caste hierarchy, conceived of as a harmonious organic unity in which each part, from the highest to the lowest, is necessary to the well-being of the whole: a few workers and managers talk like this. In this model the broad categories of workers would correspond to castes, clearly ranked, and with lesser gradations within each unit, so that the hierarchy is continuous all the way down. The possibility of moving up one unit is quite compatible with caste, because traditional caste – unlike apartheid – does not exclude some regulated movement across caste boundaries; e.g. hypergamy, or the customary ways of translating wealth into status by claiming that one's caste is really a subcaste of a high one. As L. Dumont says,

16 Dore, *British factory – Japanese factory*, p. 78.

53

'there is no absolute distinction between what happens inside and outside a caste group'; and, elsewhere, 'the caste boundary is only one more marked cleavage among others.'[17]

But it is really too simple and plausible to see the factory organization as a carry-over from traditional hierarchical thinking, when it can easily be explained as an adaptation of a western model to conditions of educated unemployment and shortage of specific factory skills. There is only a *market* for scarce skills like tool and die making; the mass of the work force are semi-skilled men, who need some education to understand the training and may acquire a skill later. Within each category, a worker's skill or productivity or usefulness probably grows over time.

Promotion

Promotion from grade to grade sometimes means moving into a new skill category; sometimes reclassification of a whole group of workers as a result of union demands; and, most often, promotion on seniority. The grade structure is similar in all four factories, and comparisons are possible.

The whole random sample average one promotion for every 5.66 years' service (see table 23). Almost everyone can expect at least one

TABLE 23. *Promotions (grade to grade) and years of service (random sample)*

Number of promotions	Years of service				
	0–4	5–9	10–14	15–19	20–4
None	78%	20%	2%	1%	–
1	18	39	28	8	13%
2	4	29	35	29	31
3	–	10	24	35	25
4	0+	1	10	22	16
5	–	1	1	5	9
6	–	0+	–	–	6
Proportion of whole sample	27%	32%	26%	12%	3%

NOTE: 65 per cent of the random sample of 1134 workers worked in the public sector, 35 per cent in the private.

[17] *Hierarchy and marriage alliance in South Indian kinship, Occasional Papers of the Royal Anthropological Institute*, 7, 1957, p. 4; 'Marriage in India', *Contributions to Indian Sociology*, 7 (1964), 77–98 (p. 83).

promotion after ten years, but he is likely to become frustrated and resentful much earlier. Managements can serve warning notices for bad work, persistent absence or other breaches of the rules, but can dismiss a worker only after a long procedure laid down by law. After a number of warning notices, the worker – or the union – can appeal to an industrial tribunal, with the power to order his reinstatement; unions can generally be relied on to act directly against 'victimization' of members.[18] In practice it is very difficult for managements to sack anyone, except for assaults on other workers or constant absence from work.[19]

Personnel officers say promotion depends on seniority and merit. Merit means efficiency, 'attitude', conduct and paper qualifications: it is assessed by confidential reports from supervisors, and trade tests which may be an alternative to paper qualifications. In the lower grades, promotion depends mainly on seniority; in the higher grades, merit before seniority. So union agreements lay down, for example, that for a skilled vacancy the three most senior candidates should be considered on merit, or that a proportion of skilled posts should be filled by promotion from lower grades and the rest by outside recruitment. Some firms (especially in the public sector) release workers for part- or full-time training at institutes or other firms, or arrange evening classes for workers who hope to learn a skill and to pass a trade examination set by an outside body.

Managements insist that promotion should remain their prerogative, but in fact they are bound by union agreements which lay down detailed criteria for promotion, and by union support for particular workers who are denied promotion. Generally the managers appear to play safe and avoid conflict with the unions.

Workers say their chances of promotion depend largely on attracting the attention of officers and foremen, whether by good work, 'obedience' (showing respect and not asking questions), belonging to the same caste or language community, bribery of factory or union officers, or even doing odd jobs in managers' houses (this is alleged,

[18] Thus in 1964 and 1965, 27 per cent of strikes were about 'personnel and retrenchment' (*Indian labour year book 1965* (Delhi, 1967), p. 109).

The *Report of the National Commission on Labour*, pp. 247–51 describes the laws and conventions about layoff and retrenchment (Factories Act, 1948; Industrial Disputes Act, 1947, amended in 1965; Code of Discipline; Model Grievance Procedure; etc.), their working, and the attitudes of managements and unions.

[19] In one large sample factory, five men had been dismissed in the previous three months: three for organized violence, two for persistent absence. Workers saw this as evidence of a new tough line taken by the management. In other factories, unions have threatened – and in some cases, successfully taken – strike action to prevent dismissals on the same grounds.

but I have no real evidence that it happens). Promotion *ought* to depend on seniority and the quality of one's work: merit, as a criterion for promotion, is more suspect than seniority, because it depends on the judgment (or favouritism) of the management, while seniority cannot be argued about. Men recruited some ten years ago emphasize the value of experience, since they were recruited before paper qualifications became so important and before there were so many chances to get them. But some skilled workers complain that they are both qualified and experienced but cannot get the promotion they deserve, because of union agreements which give too much weight to seniority: public sector workers say their chances would be better in the private sector, though in fact the situation there is almost the same. All factories reward workers who suggest useful innovations, and a surprising number of my informants have received small sums, perhaps Rs 150. But this seems to make only a slight difference to the promotion chances of the workers concerned.

The unions are caught between pressures from most of their members, who want promotion on seniority before merit, and from managements, who emphasize merit. This management pressure may be seen either as a legitimate desire to reward good work, or as a plot to make workers dependent on the arbitrary favour of officers. Each union advocates some compromise between these principles as its policy, generally with the emphasis on seniority. Union officials themselves may be in an ambiguous position: many of them are skilled men who stand to gain by a policy of promotion on merit, but publicly they have to defend the union line on seniority.

The union may take up the case ('individual grievance') of a worker denied promotion, or a demand by a group of workers ('group grievance') for a particular job title to be re-evaluated and transferred to a higher grade. In such cases I do not know how thorough the 'job evaluation' is, but I think the result depends on union–management bargaining rather than the job itself. Or a number of workers (say the twenty most senior men in one job) may be promoted together to a job title in a higher grade: the structure does not change.

Some supplement their earnings by moonlighting – taking a second job in a friend's metalwork shop, setting type for a private press, keeping a grocery shop, or hiring equipment to set up a workshop with a view to making this a full-time business if it succeeds. Moonlighting is forbidden, and a few workers have been sacked for 'multiple employment'. Some ways of making extra money are quite open: for instance, running an insurance agency or a 'chit fund' (rotating credit association).

A skilled or ambitious worker who is not prepared to wait for promotion or to start his own business will see his best chance in moving to another factory, probably a new one. This is possible (though not easy) in Bangalore, because new factories are opening there (or were in 1971). It is harder – but still possible, with luck or influence – for semi-skilled or unskilled men to move on; but most firms now prefer school-leavers for these jobs. The gain from changing jobs must be enough to compensate for loss of entitlement to retirement gratuity, after ten or fifteen years' service.

Workers in one sample factory are at a disadvantage here, because their factory is the only one of its kind in India and few of the skills are easily transferable; but this firm provides the best opportunities for workers to jump the seniority queue by the other method, which is to take evening classes for a diploma and qualify for promotion to technical assistant'. Training in a factory abroad leads to promotion; but some (not all) married men are reluctant to go, because it means one to three years' separation from their families.

Almost everyone assumes that a man will change jobs if the pay is good enough and the job equally secure. Some managements (not those of the sample factories) complain of a turnover problem, and public sector industries in Bangalore are supposed to co-ordinate their response to wage demands to avoid poaching labour from each other: but they expect a man will go where his chances are best. As one private sector general manager said, the firm expects 'loyalty', but only for as long as a worker is with the firm: they would not hold it against someone that he leaves or joins them to improve his prospects. A few men are legally bound – or think they are morally bound – to stay for some years after special training at the firm's expense, but not after ordinary training in factory skills. When turnover is quite low, most firms expect to break even by taking each other's ex-trainees; and the law compels them to train more apprentices than they can employ.

Except in special cases, a worker can usually stay with the same firm *if he wants to,* and most of them probably will; but neither workers nor management see the firm as 'an organic community which admits selected recruits to life membership' (Dore, p. 222). If there is such a community, it is the whole organized sector in the city or the state, where managements are in touch with each other (and even pass on recruits to each other), workers see their careers and union federations organize.

57

Pay

Take-home pay is made up of basic salary (for the worker's grade and step), overtime, large allowances (mostly flat-rate) and bonuses (partly in proportion to basic pay), less deductions. Median basic pay in the four factories ranges from Rs 170 to Rs 230 a month, but this does not reflect real differences in earnings because of the wide variation in bonuses and allowances. Basic pay is a useful measure of differences within a factory, not between factories. Women get the same rates as men; and although there are few women in highly skilled jobs (and fewer women officers), the median pay for men and women workers in the four factories is about the same.

The biggest single allowance is Dearness Allowance (DA), a flat rate of about Rs 90–100 added to all salaries except very high ones:[20] thus one firm pays Rs 90 to all employees (except trainees) whose salary + DA totals less than Rs 800 (so that all salaries are below Rs 710, or over Rs 800). DA is negotiated between unions and managements, in some cases with a provision that it shall go up automatically, with every one-point rise in the official cost of living index ('Simla scale').

The other big addition to salary is annual bonus, which may vary from year to year and is supposed to depend on production (though in fact it is more a bargaining counter for unions and managements). It ranges from 11 per cent of annual basic pay plus DA in one factory, to 25 per cent in another (in past years it has been much lower). On top of this are direct and indirect (or group) incentive bonuses; overtime (for those who can get it); house rent allowances (in some firms: in the two public sector firms, only for workers living outside the subsidized townships); special allowances for certain jobs (shift allowance, heat treatment allowance); and any fringe benefits the management has conceded to the union, as an alternative to higher wages (which would affect bonuses, and are a more obvious breach of employers' solidarity or public sector wage restraint). Thus one union, during my field-work, persuaded the management to pay a small education allowance to workers with children at school. Other fringe benefits are gratuity

---

[20] 'The practice of paying dearness allowances (D.A.), a practice developed during World War II to meet a rapid increase in the cost of living without permanently inflating the wage bill, has grown to such proportions that in many cases differences in the D.A. alone are responsible for variations among the companies in wage levels ... The general effect of the D.A. system is to obscure wage differentials based upon skill levels and experience.' Lambert, *Workers, factories and social change*, p. 115.

(paid after ten or fifteen years' service); employers' contribution to Employees' State Insurance and the Provident Fund; cheap or interest-free loans (one public sector firm has an allocation of scooters – which are hard to get – and gives its employees interest-free loans to buy them); subsidized canteen meals; free buses or a bicycle allowance; and so on. Table 24 shows how allowances and bonuses reduce the effect of differences in basic pay; the proportions of permanent, temporary etc. workers in the same factory are in table 25.

TABLE 24. *Workers, grades and salaries in one private factory (permanent employees only)*

Grade	Basic salary scale (Rs/month)[a]	Proportion of workers (%)	Median basic salary (Rs)	Median basic salary + Rs 90 Dearness Allowance + 25% annual bonus (Rs)[b]	DA + bonus, as a proportion of basic Salary (%)
I (unskilled)	100–5–120– 10–200	11	125	269	115
II (semi-skilled)	120–10–240	31	130	275	112
III (skilled)	150–15–330	33	195	356	83
IV (skilled)	175–17.50–385	14	227.50	397	75
V (skilled)	200–20–440	7	280	463	65
VI (skilled)	230–22.50–500	3	365	569	56
VII (senior supervisors)	300–25–450– EB–30–630	3	465	694	49
Total			180	338	88

NOTE: The sample was 600 workers.

[a] Each grade has 13 steps. 300–25–450–EB–30–630 means Rs 300 rising by steps of Rs 25 to Rs 450, then an efficiency bar, then rising by steps of Rs 30 to Rs 630. Trainees get Rs 70, or Rs 100 if they have previous training: no bonus or DA. Officers' salaries are fixed individually.

Excluding other allowances. Since most of these are flat rate, they would reduce the differences still more. There are no other production bonuses in this factory.

TABLE 25. *Total work force of the same factory,*
by conditions of employment (permanent,
temporary, etc.)

Permanent employees earning less than Rs 500/month (basic)	81%
Probationers and temporary workers	10
Full-term apprentices	3
Officers and others earning over Rs 500 (basic)	5

NOTE: The sample was 716 workers. The date was 17 months earlier than table 24.

Deductions are for Employees' State Insurance and the Provident Fund, loan repayment, canteen tickets, optional life insurance, and income tax for workers earning over Rs 5000 a year (some think it wrong that ordinary workers should pay income tax – even Rs 4 on a basic Rs 300 a month).

None of these factories pays piece-work rates, though in some cases a worker can earn a bonus related either to his production, or to qualities like attendance and 'efficiency'. (Thus one firm pays a monthly bonus to certain workers who are '70 per cent efficient'.) Other bonuses are related to the production of the whole factory, or a group of workers, but in fact are fixed by collective bargaining and cannot be reduced without causing unrest or strikes. At least two of the four firms have had strikes over production targets set by time-and-motion men.

Although earnings in a particular grade are only loosely related to productivity, this does not mean that there are no monetary incentives to raise output, or that workers are not inclined to do so for other reasons. In spite of the seniority doctrine, a hard worker improves his chances of promotion or double increments; and workers who suggest useful innovations are rewarded directly. (One man says he has received Rs 1500 in all.) And the aspiring lower-middle class most of them belong to has a self-image of conscientious work, even when their own work is hard and dull. Skill, learning and application are qualities they admire in others; they are production conscious; their commitment to India's industrial future is more than rhetoric. Union militants, communists, and those who are hostile to the management of their own factories, share these ideals with the others.

The working day is usually eight hours, with a half-hour break for lunch in the canteen: some departments work shifts (but women may not work night shifts, by law). The working week is generally six days, sometimes with shorter hours on Saturdays; and although unions have included a five-day week in their lists of demands, they have not pressed for it, and one union leader thinks his members would prefer longer annual holidays. Annual leave varies from fourteen days in one private firm (with a further seven days' casual leave, which can be taken at short notice for weddings etc., and six days' paid sick leave) to thirty days in the public sector.

All workers, except those on the highest salaries, are covered by Employees' State Insurance (ESI). The worker and his family are entitled to free medical consultations at ESI clinics throughout the city, hospital treatment, sickness allowance for a limited period, maternity benefit and benefits in case of complete or partial disablement. Workers covered by ESI lose their entitlement to Workmen's Compensation from the company in case of accident. Factories will often find alternative light work for a disabled employee, at the same basic pay: but he loses chances of promotion and incentive bonuses, and of course he becomes more dependent on the firm. One public sector factory recruits and trains blind workers, who use specially adapted machines. All the sample factories (in glaring contrast to the unorganized sector) appear to take accident prevention seriously, and the unions supplement the work of the government factory inspectors.

Various factory schemes, organized on union or management initiative with a contribution from the firm, give additional aid when the ESI allowance runs out after eight weeks, and in hard cases. Thus workers at one public sector factory pay Rs 2 to become life members of a Social Welfare Society, which guarantees monthly payments to disabled ex-workers. And all firms make subsidized welfare loans.

The ESI system is imperfect; workers complain of queues and cursory treatment at clinics, and delays in getting accident compensation – here the unions can help. But it is much better than the services available to unorganized sector workers and their families: mainly charitable clinics or doctors who do not charge poor patients, and treatment in the overcrowded free wards of hospitals.

There is no unemployment pay. The worker's Provident Fund contributions are refunded when he retires or dies, with interest and a matching contribution from the employer (paid in full after a number of years' service). The only other way a worker can make provision for his family and old age is by taking out a policy with the government Life Insurance Corporation, or investing in a house or land. Very few have long-term cash savings.

I said most workers are production conscious and admire hard conscientious work. These ideals are part of the culture, taken for granted (as they are, for example, in Japan, but not so much in England).[21] This does not mean everyone finds his own job satisfying or meaningful, or enjoys the social atmosphere of the factory, or accepts the legitimacy of the management structure (to the extent that the Japanese do). One can be 'alienated' from one's work, and the organization one does it in, but still 'committed' to industrialism as potentially a good way of life; and I think this attitude is quite common.

Much factory work anywhere is dull, hard and repetitive. Some people do not mind work that is merely repetitive, like adding small components on an assembly line in two of the sample factories. One girl complained that she had been taken off the assembly line – where work was easy and she could chat – for inspection work, which required attention. A press operator spends all day, every day, operating a press with his foot to punch a metal case out of a moving strip, with occasional ten-minute breaks: he wants more money, but says the work is all right. Others hate this kind of work and do it because they see no alternative.

A young machine operator fills holes in a plate with identical small components (with slight variations between batches).[22] The machine grinds them, they fall out of the plate, and someone takes them away. He gets a production bonus. Sometimes the machine is not properly adjusted, the components

---

[21] Dore, *British factory – Japanese factory*, quotes a British shop steward (p. 246)/ 'If I were to go down to the local and admit that I take a pride in my work, I'd be laughed at.' Dore comments: 'Those who have the kind of routine jobs in which it is hard to take any kind of pride have probably made up a more dominant majority of the working class over more generations in Britain than in Japan, so that their natural view of work as purely an unpleasant means of earning money has become the dominant cultural assumption of working class society' (p. 246). 'The work atmosphere in Japanese factories is such that people are pleased (not, like the British shop steward quoted on p. 246, embarrassed) to acknowledge that they get some satisfaction out of their work and some feeling of pride from the exercise of their skills' (p. 277).

[22] I have to describe some jobs in a roundabout way: if the 'components' were named, this would identify the factory.

62

come out wrong, and he feels very upset. He would like to work in another factory, but sees no chance of moving because he has no important friends to recommend him. The way to get promotion is to work hard and ask no questions: say 'yes, yes' to supervisors and foremen even if they are wrong.

Or the work is hard, hot or exhausting, like heat treatment or lifting heavy pieces of metal, so that a man is worn out by lunch time. Young men do not mind so much, if there is a prospect of easier work: like a skilled man who spent his first eighteen months unloading and installing machinery in the new factory – by the evening he was so sweaty that no one liked to sit by him on the bus. But men of 30 or 35 who are still doing heavy work – even skilled, interesting work – feel they should be made inspectors or transferred to clerical work (a man who had been a turner for eleven years said 'man is not a machine' – he could work hard and produce more as a planner or inspector); or they think of working until they qualify for gratuity and then trying something else, like a shop.

The most satisfying (and best paid) manual jobs are those of craftsmen who work more or less independently, like lathe operators or toolmakers who make a component to exact specifications and generally without constant supervision. These men take pleasure in describing their daily routine in detail: the precise tolerances allowed in centreless grinding; the chemistry of electroplating; the constant variety of components a lathe operator makes; how a group of two or three assemble a large machine from drawings and check the components for faults, putting precision and quality before speed and quantity; the draftsmen's work, converting designers' drawings into drawings the assembly workers can use ('we also think a little bit, whether it works or not'). Again and again, men said they enjoyed, or would like to do, work that is skilled and varied, where they learn something new, and promotion chances are good until one reaches the top of a particular skilled grade.

But most of the sample workers are neither repetitive assembly-line workers nor independent craftsmen. They carry out one of a series of operations which require some skill and may vary slightly, either from one piece of work to the next, or at least from one production run to the next, depending on the orders the company gets. Or they set one or more automatic machines and monitor the product, correct small faults, and report major ones to the supervisor. One man sets an automatic machine to do a job – this always involves 'new problems' – then switches it on and it does the job by itself ('like magic – that's why I like that job'). But men doing this kind of work more often regard it as the price one pays for working in a 'good' factory, with high wages and security: on the whole they see the necessity of their work, they accept the production goals of the management whether they get on well with the management staff or not. But they do not pretend the work itself is satisfying: the work is 'sometimes interesting ... but we have been forced to do it, haven't we?'; 'I *make* myself interested'; 'The worker need not know anything, either about the machine or about the part he is manufacturing; then gradually, he has to pick up the job in his own interest'; (or, from a boring-machine operator, evidently an old joke in English:) 'We can't say [it is] boring, because we are all borers!' It is best if one can move around the factory a bit, or at least talk to friends while working. An overhead crane operator manages to keep up continuous conversation by shouting down to men on the shop floor below. Some workers value the companionship most of all, and regard the ideal factory as a system of warm human relationships.

The supervisors, foremen, chargehands and group leaders, who allocate the work, give informal training and sometimes do the most skilled or difficult jobs themselves, are of the same middle-class background as the educated skilled and semi-skilled men. (So are the 'officers', very often; but they keep more to themselves socially, and their contacts with workers tend to be functional and correct.) Supervisors emphasize the close friendly relations they enjoy with the men under them – like a family – and play down their role as agents of management with sanctions at their disposal. In fact some of them are elected union officials. Yet workers say some supervisors keep to themselves, not sitting and chatting with workers in their spare time, and eating separately (this is partly because some supervisors may mind the machines while workers are at lunch). They can initiate disciplinary action: warning notices from the management, leading to eventual dismissal, for laziness, absenteeism, inefficiency or violence. But disciplinary action is cumbersome, slow and likely to lead to union trouble. The supervisor's real sanctions – and the ones workers talk most often about – are rewards: the power to recommend promotion or double increments, or simply to give a word of encouragement. A supervisor who treats workers rudely or takes them for granted will be condemned in tones of real moral indignation. So although the Japanese style of earnest moral exhortation to pull together for the common good of employees at all levels is not taken nearly so seriously, there still seems to be a common assumption that the firm ought to be a moral community, of human and not merely functional relations – though in reality it *is not* what it ought to be.

The unions

Women workers

With few exceptions, I met women workers only in their husbands' company. One of the four factories employs a high proportion of women (one-third of the work force), mostly on assembly-line work or in the office, and maintains a crèche for their young children when they return after their three months' maternity leave. Other women leave children at home with relatives, neighbours or paid servants.

The idea that unmarried women and workers' wives should go to work is taken more and more for granted. Men ask their parents to arrange a marriage for them with girls who can continue earning after marriage – or the men ask the girls themselves, without regard to caste, something that is still unusual but no longer always scandalous, as it would have been in the early 1960s. Nor is it thought odd that women should work beside men in some departments, under male supervision. But the limits of propriety are still close: the one woman 'draftsman' says the men in her office treat her as a sister, but she never goes among the men on the factory floor to discuss design problems, and so she cannot get promotion. Women keep to themselves in the canteen, play a minor part in most clubs and then only in the shadow of their husbands, and take little part in the union beyond attending general meetings and voting.

The social barriers which keep women out of male conversation and decision making seem likely to weaken rapidly. In the urban lower-middle class many workers come from, the trend is to educate girls for a possible career combined with marriage – and not just 'feminine' careers, like teaching and typing. I know of at least two girls who were sent to Germany for training in skilled trades, and a worker's wife with a civil engineering diploma who is looking for suitable work. Women are beginning to compete with men, not only for assembly-line and office work, but for skilled, supervisory management jobs. Such women are still a small minority: but how much longer will career women keep to the company of their own sex?

The unions

One factory, one union, is the usual pattern: there are no craft unions with members from different factories. This is all right for organized sector workers, since each factory union is in a strong position to negotiate on behalf of all permanent employees: too much emphasis on craft or skill differences would weaken them. But it leaves unorganized sector workers largely unprotected: most attempts to organize unions among them have failed.

Three of the four sample factories have one union each, containing most manual and clerical workers except trainees, temporary workers and supervisory staff. One factory has two rival unions, both confined to the factory, divided along political not craft lines.

The law lays down conditions for union recognition, registration of agreements, arbitration by industrial tribunals and industrial action. The formalities for starting a legal strike are so cumbersome that many strikes are technically 'illegal', and a wise union leader knows how far illegal action can go without putting the union at a disadvantage in the legalistic process of negotiation. Every union needs a legal adviser, or an outside 'leader' with some legal knowledge. At least some union officials must be able to understand legal agreements and to argue a case before industrial tribunals; and all this paper work is done in English.

Most Indian unions belong to national federations, linked with political parties (especially the pro-Congress INTUC and the communist AITUC). Two of the sample factory unions are 'independent', one is in AITUC, and the rival unions in the other factory belong to INTUC and AITUC.

The biggest federation is the Indian National Trade Union Congress (INTUC), which supports the Congress Party. After the Congress split in 1969, most INTUC activists supported the new, or ruling, Congress (known as Congress (R) to distinguish it from the old, or organization, Congress (O)).

The other big federation is the All-India Trade Union Congress (AITUC), which supports the Communist Party of India (CPI); but some office-bearers in AITUC unions, and many members, do not support the Party. The AITUC leader for Mysore State is a communist member of the state Legislative Assembly and stood for the Bangalore City constituency in the 1971 General Election. Members of his unions organized his campaign from their offices. He was heavily defeated, partly because his main support (and his Assembly constituency) was in industrial suburbs outside this parliamentary constituency, and partly because many factory workers admired him as a union leader but voted 'for Indira' and the new Congress.

Smaller federations are the socialist Hind Mazdoor Sabha (HMS), with some important unions in Bangalore; and two with little industrial support, which are really industrial wings of parties – the Centre for Indian Trade Unions (CITU) which broke away from AITUC to support the Communist Party of India (Marxist) (CPI(M) or CPM), and the Bharatiya Mazdoor Sangh, closely identified with the Jan Sangh. A union will often join a federation because the local leader is known as a strong negotiator, not because of his political opinions: as leader, president or legal adviser to the union, he can guide it through the legal thickets of negotiation, and may be able to use political connexions to the members' advantage. If he fails to deliver the union will drop him: three of the sample unions have done this.

Each union, except the smallest one, has its office in a room or small house, in most cases subsidized by the management. There is no permanent paid staff, apart from a few 'outsiders' in the federation offices. In each union, committee members do the paper work. Usually there is someone in the office in the evenings, or at weekends, but not regularly. Union officials and committee members – especially young unmarried ones – use it as a clubhouse to meet friends and talk. So do a few other workers who know them, or who want to discuss grievances about promotion and so on; but most men with grievances go through the committee members in their own departments. The committee meets formally at least once a month. At least once a year there is a general meeting of all members, except in very large firms.

Almost everyone – managers and workers alike – accepts that workers will and should belong to a union. The Indian unions' struggle for recognition was won long ago in the modern organized sector (though one sample union registered secretly, because its leaders were afraid the management of the new factory might try to keep unions out). Now only the small employers are in a position to hold out against unions. Indeed some large private employers seem to prefer unions belonging to the communist AITUC, which has a reputation for driving a hard bargain but keeping its agreements. Even communist unions do not think their independence is compromised if the management pays the rent for their offices, or gives them an easy loan to buy an office. Other unions get other kinds of help: easy jobs for union officials, leaving them time for union work; in one factory, technical training abroad; and so on.

The main union activities have already been mentioned: informal negotiation with factory officers, and occasional formal meetings with management, on individual grievances over promotion and disciplinary action; discussion of general questions of promotion policy, pay and allowances, and working conditions; and (in some factories) organizing social events like sports days and variety shows, with a management subsidy.

Each union has its own style, reflecting its size and history and the ideas of the people who have built it up – often, one man. Some unions are led or influenced by men with equalitarian ideals, who see union action as a stage in the struggle to liberate all the working class, including those outside the organized sector; others by men with an ideology of loyalty to a paternalistic management, or the divine right of the middle class to secure employment. Some unions are run on strictly pragmatic lines, without much ideology beyond the need for honest efficient organization in the members' interest; some are riven by language or caste rivalry; and some are dominated by careerists, men who are alleged to line their own pockets, rig union elections, sell jobs, and keep all the advantages like quick promotion for themselves and their friends. Union officials are not paid, and do the work because of idealism, because they find it interesting or because of some other advantage.

It would be too simple to see the unions just as networks of transactions, in which everyone maximizes his interest. This 'transactional' view is either circular (if any human purposes count as interests, it is not much use observing that people always maximize *something*) or plainly wrong. One can only make sense of people's behaviour on the assumption that their motives are a mixture of self-interest and many kinds of values and ideological considerations; and the relation of ideology (a whole world-view, from which particular judgments follow) to group interest is indirect, long-term and complicated. Some ideological rhetoric should be taken seriously, some is meant to deceive others who take it seriously; but if no one took it seriously there would be no point in using it.

The styles of union operation represent different solutions to the practical and ideological problems of advancing members' (and officials') interests in a situation where factory workers are a social élite. The tension between interest and ideology is most acute in unions with a strong equalitarian ideology, mainly the communist ones. Their active members are often idealists who sincerely want a classless society; anyway, the unions depend for useful support on the federation and party, many of whose members are in less privileged parts of the organized sector or outside it. The solution is to present the militant (though well-paid) factory workers as the spearhead of the working class, whose victories will strengthen the hand of less fortunate workers fighting for better pay and conditions, and who can lead the struggle for socialism. So workers in AITUC unions use their union offices as communist committee rooms at election times, and canvass in the neighbourhood. But the same skilled, communist workers, who demand wholesale nationalization

68

on principle, say their own pay and working conditions are better in private firms.

This example of a one-day strike shows how the union leaders' priorities may differ from those of the membership:

The union in a private factory had agreed with the management on a new incentive bonus scale, and the firm prepared to pay it. Then union officials asked for further clarification; the management said the issue was settled and could not be reopened; but since clearly it was to be reopened anyway, the accounts department would pay for the current month at the rates calculated, and make any adjustments the next month. A notice went up, giving details of the bonus to be paid, and the union officials took this to mean their request had been refused.

At noon the committee members called their departments out on strike. A few non-unionists went on working, and a foreman who did so was pushed away from the machine by angry workers. Since the two senior Directors had to leave by plane, the personnel officer was left to settle the strike. In the afternoon, the unionists called in their 'leader' – a full-time AITUC worker, who talked to the personnel officer, then told the union executive they were in the wrong. He persuaded them – and then a mass meeting of workers – to go back to work the same afternoon.

This left two issues to settle when the Directors came back: the union demanded full payment for the hours of the strike, and settled for about half; and it persuaded the management (again through the leader's good offices) to drop disciplinary charges against three workers who had pushed the foreman, on condition that they apologized to him.

Two months later the union held its annual general body meeting. The leader congratulated the union on their achievements – they had even managed to get pay for the period of an illegal strike, which no other Bangalore union had been able to do – but warned them not to push their demands too far, because this might rebound on them. Pointedly he talked about the struggle of the underpaid mill workers; thanked the union for Rs 1000, which he would give to the Party; and asked for more contributions to support full-time AITUC workers like himself.

Another variant of equalitarian ideology is reformist and gradualist: unions should work to eliminate big differences of income and status between factory workers but cannot do much, for the time being, to help those without factory jobs. In the long run, these people will benefit by all-round industrial progress, middle-class 'social work', and political changes. This ideology shades into what I have called 'the divine right of the middle class' to jobs and housing and good schools: where the middle class (or skilled factory workers) lead, others will follow.

Whether a union has an 'ideological' or a 'pragmatic' style, the ways in which it can work most effectively depend largely on the kind of management it has to deal with. In very big firms, especially in the public sector, the real decision makers are far away, managements cannot commit themselves without referring to high authority, reaction from that authority is slow and uncertain and affected by large-scale politics: so political influence may be more effective than plant-level negotiation and industrial action. In small firms, especially private ones, the decision makers are visible, reaction is quick and represents a straight calculation of interest, tempered by mild benevolence and the common values shared by management and middle-class workers.

Thus the union in one private factory is split between a strongly ideological faction (the 'paternalists', see pp. 88–95) and a pragmatic faction, of men who built up the union and are used to working in a more 'transactional' way. During my fieldwork, each faction put up a full list of candidates for all union offices, with its party symbol on the ballot paper, and the 'paternalists' won. The 'paternalists' stress the common interests of management and workers; they are inclined to militant neo-Hinduism, and the Jan Sangh party.

In the other private factory (the smallest, and the one where the six-hour strike took place), the union is led by a group of young skilled men, some of them idealistic communists, but mostly men with good prospects of rising within the factory or managing their family's land or small business if they leave. The union belongs to AITUC for convenience rather than ideology. There are no clear factions in it. Elections for union office are about personalities rather than issues, and the ordinary committee members are usually elected unopposed by their departments.

One public sector factory has an effective, pragmatic leadership, under the control of one graduate worker and his friends (see pp. 98–9). The union is independent of all federations. It has a hierarchy of officials (general council, executive committee, 'office-bearers') to deal with grievances at every level and to handle negotiations at the top, not only at plant level but by mobilizing political connexions higher up. These men know how to use the legal negotiation and arbitration machinery to their members' best advantage, the right moment to resort to a 'legal' strike or to appeal to a minister. They are incorruptible, conscientious, well meaning, and generally support the Congress Party's kind of socialism.[23] They believe national progress

---

[23] This union organizes a full social life for its members. In 1966 this included an elocution contest on the theme 'Intermarriage as a means to National Unity'.

depends on a strong public sector. In the long run, they say, this will bring relative equality and security to everyone; in the meantime, the government (including public sector management) has a duty to protect the living standards of hard-working middle-class people like themselves. (Speaking English, they tend to call themselves 'middle class'; the communists say 'working class'; both mean the same in this context.) There are no 'parties' in this union, and the leader tries to keep some check on language factionalism.

In the other public sector factory the contrast between ideological and transactional styles appears in the bitter rivalry between two unions: a strongly ideological communist one, whose active members sacrifice their career prospects (pp. 96–8), and a 'recognized' union, with no ideology to speak of. Men who know what is good for them join the 'recognized' union (though some say privately they would join the other if they could). Since the communist union cannot negotiate officially with the management, its leaders concentrate on winning control of the co-operative and other elected bodies in the factory township, and sometimes appear before disciplinary committees on behalf of workers threatened with suspension. There is such bitterness between the two unions that it is hard to check allegations against facts, or to judge the truth of highly coloured accounts of violence, victimization, dismissals, exploitation of communal differences, rigging of elections and corruption.

As soon as someone becomes 'permanent' (i.e. not 'temporary', an apprentice, or a trainee), the union committee member for the department asks him or her to join, and almost everyone does. Subscriptions are low, because the unions have no full-time staff, usually get management subsidies in the form of cheap office premises and time off for union work, and have no strike funds – though they quite often call strikes. The first advantage of membership is help with individual grievances, especially promotion, and some protection against dismissal and disciplinary action. Inevitably this leads to charges that committee members and union officials are biased, and push the cases of their friends – or sometimes their language group – more vigorously than those of other workers. And certainly one's chances of promotion are better if one knows a committee member personally: I have heard the committee of a small union discussing whose cases deserved to be pushed – on grounds of seniority and 'efficiency' – in terms which suggested close personal knowledge of the people concerned. The unskilled workers, sweepers, watchmen etc. have their own committee members, generally men with little education, who collect subscriptions and go to committee meetings, but leave the talking to younger, educated members. Union elections arouse a good deal of short-lived enthusiasm: candidates' friends distribute handbills with slogans ('A symbol of unity and humanity'; 'Fighting for real workers' freedom') or occasionally the manifesto of a faction. The poll is high, because workers get time off to vote; for the same reason, general meetings are well attended. If the union calls a strike, most respond willingly – they will sacrifice pay or their comfort in stay-in strikes that last for days, without complaint – but they leave the decision to begin and end strikes to the leaders. Most workers' relation to the union is 'transactional' most of the time: the union provides a service when needed. In return it occasionally asks for sacrifice, solidarity and enthusiasm.

The union leaders, and their most active supporters, are mostly educated, younger workers, of middle-class urban or rich peasant origin, of any caste, and often immigrants from Tamil Nadu or Kerala. Their social backgrounds and attitudes are not very different from those of the management: some of them have relatives in factory managements or in offices, and in a few cases this is how they got their jobs.

To some extent, all the unions show signs of a citadel mentality: the lower-middle class closing ranks to defend its precarious privileges and its relative security in a situation where the prospects are uncertain for everyone. Union members have to think not only of job security, but of prospects for their families. Yet the citadel is not of their making. The unions can use political influence to maintain the value of wages or to prevent layoffs, but their actions probably make little difference to the fate of workers outside the organized sector – whether they care about these people or not.

Whole factories might close down, the economy might collapse, revolutions and upheavals are a constant possibility; yet factory workers like to believe that in spite of everything, economic development and stability will continue, more and more people will benefit by it, and India will become more like a prosperous and relatively classless western society – Germany, for example.

Other associations

Urban South Indians are great 'joiners': the old informal groups of friends meeting in front of someone's house, bhajana (hymn-singing) groups, and traditional factions and caste networks, are transformed into clubs and associations with written constitutions and elected officers, often a name on a signboard, permanent premises and headed notepaper.

Some are based in city neighbourhoods. 'Young men's clubs' (often with middle-aged members as well) meet to play cards in a room over a café, and can sometimes be mobilized to canvass at elections. 'Social work' groups, often associated more closely with political parties like the Tamil–populist DMK, have a nucleus of hard workers who give free classes to slum children; the other members pay for a free reading room, with newspapers and paperbacks, which they use as a clubhouse and a committee room at elections. The most active associations are probably religious ones, which maintain local temples and priests, arrange weekly bhajanas and spectacular annual festivals and processions, classical concerts and harikathas (moralized telling of myths by professional religious entertainers).

Other associations are factory based (or based in a factory township, which comes to the same thing). Some public sector factories have an elaborate structure of management-inspired associations and elected bodies: co-operatives, township management committees, house-building societies, death benefit funds; even 'cultural' associations for each language group or religious minority, with a factory officer of the community as president. The official ideology is one of gradually increasing worker participation in factory affairs. Elections to these bodies can become an arena for union or political rivalries.

A more common type of association is subsidized by private or public management, and is only partly a result of management initiative. The most active are sports clubs. Factory football teams practice during working hours, and some workers are recruited because of their skill at football. 'Cultural' associations or 'fine arts clubs' are mainly dramatic societies, and very popular: they put on 'social dramas' (i.e. about social problems), comedies and variety entertainments, and tend to involve some young women as well as men.[24] Management support for clubs is a fringe benefit rather than a concerted policy of involving workers emotionally with the firm, in Japanese style.

At home: the household and its economy

Modern Bangalore is the result of rapid post-war growth around two major centres – the old city, and the British Cantonment which was separately administered until 1947 – and many minor centres which

[24] Men are still in a large majority. But in a few cases young men and women have met in dramatic clubs and married for love: this shocks some people and delights others. Love marriage is the fantasy of many young men (and women?), and the Romeo and Juliet theme is a favourite plot for 'social dramas'.

are former villages, but which keep their names, their old village families, and a self-conscious identity as 'villages' with their own temples, festivals and titular headmen. The filling between old village centres consists of straight avenues, lined with trees, and symmetrical blocks. The narrow winding streets of the centres are paved with tarmac or granite, and usually have underground drains and overhead electric wires. There are old farm houses or cottages, built of white-washed adobe or small red bricks with roofs of corrugated Mangalore tiles; sheds for the cows which still wander round the streets and graze on patches of open ground; bigger houses of local landlords and businessmen, often in garishly painted concrete; rows of one- or two-room ground-floor apartments round courtyards, built by specu-lative landlords for immigrant workers; general stores and smaller shops; and colonies of adobe huts, with thatched or corrugated iron roofs, which the very poor build for themselves on vacant sites, pay-ing the landlord a small ground rent. Bangalore has few large slums like those in Bombay or Delhi – vast areas of crowded huts without access to water or sanitation – but many smaller colonies of huts, usually between fifteen and a hundred on one site.

Some factory workers live in the middle-class areas between village centres, often renting part of a house, or a small tenement built in the back yard. A few buy houses subsidized and built by public sector factories. But most live either in the planned factory townships (which accommodate perhaps a quarter of the public sector workers) or in the expanded village centres.

The typical factory worker's house is a two-room apartment, with floors of polished red concrete, electric light, sometimes a separate tap and lavatory but often sharing with a few other families – of mixed caste, language and religion – living on the same courtyard. Almost every house has a radio; usually a table and a chair or two, though meals are eaten on the floor; sometimes beds; and sometimes an electric fan, a sewing machine, a cooker using bottled gas, and other modern appliances. There is not much room or privacy: accom-modation is plain and clean, the neighbourhood generally healthy and peaceful – certainly not a slum.[25]

Other workers live in rambling peasant houses, with accommoda-tion for a large joint family and cattle; sometimes in really cramped

---

[25] The climate has something to do with it. 'From the point of view of human comfort, the City's climate approaches ideal condition in a monsoon region . . . It is seldom muggy and never scorching' (R. L. Singh, *Bangalore: an urban survey* (Varanasi, 1964), p. 10): very different from the nerve-racking closeness of small flats in the Delhi summer.

and unhealthy conditions (though seldom in the real slums, where few inhabitants can hope for anything better than casual building labour, market work and so on); and occasionally in flats, or whole houses, where the family earnings permit a solidly middle-class life style, with well-furnished rooms, a refrigerator and a scooter parked inside the front door.

The landlords are local businessmen – often men of old peasant families, who built on their fields and sometimes became building contractors themselves; or middle-class owner–occupiers, who make ends meet by renting out part of the house; or even other factory workers.

Except for those living in factory townships, workers often live far from their factories: wherever they find accommodation at a suitable rent, usually through networks of relatives and friends working in different factories. So one finds concentrations of factory workers generally, with similar accommodation and life style, rather than workers from the same factory. This is largely because factories have their own good bus services throughout the city, and few workers have to queue for the inadequate city buses as office workers do. Factory buses are fast, quite cheap and convenient. Others go to work by bicycle, on foot or by scooter.

A minority live in the planned townships around public sector factories outside the city, five or ten kilometres from the city centre. Each township has its own parks, schools, shopping centre, places of worship, hospital, sports club and cinema. Rows of identical detached houses, with small well-kept gardens, stand along quiet lanes. The only variety is in the housing for employees at different salary levels. If you ask where someone lives, your informant may ask what work he does, and will then tell you to ask again in another part of the township. Thus in one township workers whose basic salary is under Rs 300 a month have two-room houses, with kitchen, lavatory and washing place, at a rent of Rs 16 (or 10 per cent of basic salary, if this is less). Workers earning over Rs 300 pay Rs 20 for a house with one extra room. 'Officers' have bigger houses, with lawns and garages, according to their rank.

These rents, of course, are much less than for similar accommodation in the city, and the house rent allowance paid to workers living outside the townships only fills part of the gap. So workers living in the city often say they would like a house in the township; those who have one are divided about the advantages, apart from the low rent.[26]

[26] The *Report of the National Commission on Labour*, p. 33, says employers find it difficult to satisfy the 'insistent demand from workers for a separate township'.

Thus workers say townships are quiet and peaceful, or terribly dull, like farms; away from the rush of the city and well provided with amenities, or away from the pleasing variety of city life, city entertainments, friends and relatives. If rents are low, the shops are more expensive because there is less competition. Some workers throw themselves with enthusiasm into township clubs and activities: collections for a new temple, festivals, amateur dramatics and sports, or the elected Managing Committee which some townships have. A few are alleged to rent out their township houses, having somewhere else to live, or to use them for small businesses. (I have no evidence of this.) But men who have a township house often want to buy a subsidized house in a more central area if possible.

In the case study sample, the median worker's household has five members, with two non-workers to each earning member. If married, he has a median of two children. Of the sample, 9 per cent live alone or with non-relatives, 43 per cent in nuclear families, and 47 per cent in larger family groups (e.g. nuclear family with parents, or married sons or brothers). The largest factory made its own sample survey of workers: 72 per cent had a dependent wife, 81 per cent had dependent parents (though not necessarily living with them), and the median couple had two children.

I shall sidestep the argument about whether industrialization is 'breaking up the joint family', except to observe that 'jointness' may be a traditional *ideal* rather than a traditional *practice*; and that statistics of household composition, taken at a particular point in the domestic cycle and urban growth, may give a misleading picture of the long-run ideological changes making for the reinforcement or breakup of joint family living, and of the subtle relations between joint family ideology and circumstances.[27] Men may value joint

Private factories do not seem to build townships unless they are in remote areas with no other accommodation. I do not know how far public sector policy is affected by non-economic factors, like the ideal of a self-contained and geometrically planned community as an example of 'good town planning'.

For an excellent study of a private sector township in a rural area – with practical suggestions for overcoming the dullness and social isolation of life in such places and making them real communities – see Kapadia and Devadas Pillai, *Industrialization and rural society.*

[27] The best general discussion is I. P. Desai, *Some aspects of family in Mahuva* (Bombay, 1964). There is evidence that industrial workers' families are often joint, sometimes more so than in the rural or non-industrial population: e.g. Lambert, *Workers, factories and social change*; M. S. A. Rao, 'Occupational diversification and joint household organization', *Contributions to Indian Sociology*, new series, 2 (1968), 98–111 (p. 98).

living highly, and leave their fathers' households expecting (or hoping) to set up their own joint households, yet the circumstances of the caste or the particular family may ensure that very few joint households survive; or they may value privacy and take nuclear family living as the norm, yet urban economic conditions may make joint living inevitable. So men living separately (like 'Sriinivaas', see pp. 94–5) sometimes wish they could afford a suitable house in which to live jointly with their brothers; while those in joint households may wish they could afford to move out. Typically, middle-class or skilled working-class families, if they can rent an apartment with enough rooms, settle for a loose federation between nuclear families, respecting each couple's privacy and financial independence, but with a common fund for food and rent and specific purposes. Those who cannot afford such a big place live in nuclear households if they can, perhaps with an unemployed relative until he finds work, or looking after old parents. The case study sample showed no relation between basic salary and household size.

When a household has more than one earning member, each may give his pay packet to the father or eldest brother and take back a regular amount for his own nuclear family's expenses – entertainments, little luxuries and sometimes clothes. In a few cases he simply asks the head of the family for money when he needs it (the 'traditional' way). Most commonly, each earner gives the same amount, or a proportion of his earnings, and keeps the rest. Food, fuel and rent always come from the common fund; so do any remittances to relatives, and major expenses like marriages; sometimes all clothes; and sometimes basic clothes, leaving each nuclear family to pay for more or better clothes. Some families buy all their clothes on a single outing when the annual bonus is paid.

Three brothers in a factory township managed to get houses side by side, and pulled down the fences. Their joint family, with twenty-five members, lives in two of the houses, and keeps the third (I was told) for visiting relatives and others. The eldest brother handles all the money. But this is an odd case.

Some have a share in joint family property elsewhere, usually land. They may get a small income from it, but more often they leave the income to the brothers or other relatives who work the land. A few intend to go back and farm the land themselves.

Remittances sent by city workers to rural relatives are common, and quite large. A man with a wife and child, whose pay and bonus total Rs 360, sends Rs 50 a month to his peasant father and more at festivals. A man with a wife and three children, taking home about

Rs 450, sends Rs 50 or 75 to his father, who gave up weaving because of heart trouble: now his mother supports five people by weaving. These remittances must be added to the cost (and inconvenience) of supporting relatives who move to Bangalore, to look for work or just to stay.

Very few workers have long-term savings, except forced savings in the Provident Fund. Those who can save a little for emergencies put it into chit funds, or rotating credit associations. This brings in a variable rate of interest, depending on the demand for loans, and allows the member to bid for the 'chit' or loan when he needs it.

It is hard to plan budgets more than a month ahead, partly because of inflation. Most people have just enough for regular expenses – food, rent, transport, clothes, school books, cinemas, chit fund subscriptions etc. – with little or nothing left over for major expenses, which arise because of illness, family crises and ceremonies, house repairs and so on. Any sudden expenditure forces them to borrow, from friends or relatives if they can, more often by bidding for a 'chit', taking a factory loan or turning to pawnbrokers or money-lenders. Factory workers who specialize in lending money are said to charge 10–20 per cent *monthly* interest. (I was not able to check this.)

A young Brahman says his pay is just enough, because of the careful way he plans his expenditure on the first of each month. He has no 'luxuries' and hates to borrow: but he had to take a factory loan (at 9 per cent a year) for his child's naming ceremony. He puts any savings into building a village house for his parents.

Another Brahman gave up drink and cigarettes to save money. As a shareholder in a co-operative bank, he borrowed Rs 1000 for a family ceremony, some furniture, and house repairs.

An unmarried semi-skilled worker lives in his father's joint household. The house was mortgaged to pay for his sister's wedding, and they must pay back Rs 200 a month or lose the house.

A skilled Harijan says his pay is not enough to support a large family. At the end of the month he often has to adjust – 'not exactly borrowing' – and he can get more overtime.

A union leader tells me some chit fund organizers lose or spend the money entrusted to them, and disappear from the factory to escape violence.

The same leader helped a worker to get a Rs 2000 bank loan for a small printing press, where the worker can make money in his spare time with his brother's help. It will still be hard to pay for type and overheads; but his church is making a room available rent free and he hopes to print church papers, wedding invitations etc.

The family in the caste

So who benefits from factory employees' spending? Shopkeepers and shop workers, people providing all kinds of services – washermen, cafés and cinemas, transport workers etc. Landlords – often men owning a few houses built on what was once the family farm – and a large construction industry, mostly in the hands of small contractors employing casual labourers. Servants in officers' houses. Factory workers' unemployed or underpaid relatives, including many in small towns and rural areas (a great deal of money goes out to farming families, and only a little comes in from farms in which factory workers have a share). And many others who can make a living because of the multiplier effect of factory employees' spending.

On another level, the large unorganized sector in Bangalore – especially the small engineering workshops – and the large factories are interdependent in many ways. Workshops supply the factories with components and buy second-hand machinery; workers trained and experienced in the large factories start their own workshops, while the workshops provide a reserve of men with some skill; and so on (see Lakshman).

The family in the caste

The usual worker's household is not a 'traditional' joint family. It is a nuclear family, sometimes with old parents or unemployed relatives; or it is a loose federation of nuclear families, who respect each other's privacy, pool only part of their incomes, and stay together for as long as it suits them. But sentiment, marriage and economic ties bind the household to a network of kin, often in rural areas, and to a caste spread throughout a region or state. Differences between the modern urban situation and the 'traditional' (often rural) situation are not necessarily signs of real, lasting change; but they may be, if we have more evidence of what people think and do. What does caste mean now, and how is it relevant to action?

Traditionally castes are ranked, interdependent, endogamous groups. They are separated by rules of pollution, and each caste is supposed to have its own occupation and moral duties. This is both a book view and a popular ideology. In traditional practice the rank order is clear only at the top and bottom; and caste specialization only affects a minority, because agriculture and trade have been open to all castes.

Caste ideology stresses hierarchy and interdependence. Separation, endogamy (or sometimes hypergamy) and specialization follow logically from these two principles. This is roughly L. Dumont's view:[28] I think it is correct but that Dumont largely ignores the dialectical relation between this ideology and another tradition, which is critical of caste and stresses equality and choice. If caste is losing most of its moral and practical significance (as I suggested on pp. 33–4), this may be a continuation of an old anticaste tradition in new circumstances.

I had to be especially careful in interpreting what people said about caste and marriage. They know foreigners have no caste and often dislike caste, and sometimes it was obvious workers were saying what they thought I wanted to hear, or defending caste, or showing their anticaste credentials. And my family life aroused curiosity, especially among young men who are fascinated by the idea of love marriage. I had to judge what people really meant, in the light of what I already knew about life in Bangalore.

Caste is thought to affect – and sometimes does affect – recruitment and promotion in factories. So do other kinds of 'community': religion and language. But caste is no longer plausible as a thorough-going religious ideology, justifying all social and economic relations as parts of a divinely established hierarchy. The main public ideology – not just the language of politics and unions, but much ordinary talk – tends to stress moral and social equality. The status inequalities that count depend on jobs, income, life style, manners and education. Where these things go with caste rank, this is usually because some castes had more access to education and good jobs in the past – a situation that will not last, because effective caste job-finding networks are not stable or confined to high castes. The idea of hierarchical interdependence survives among workers who have an ideology of loyalty to an organization, but without reference to caste, and with the assumption that social mobility is possible – that there is always room at the top.

The old rules about contact between castes are irrelevant in many situations for most people – in all situations, for some people. Almost everyone will eat with Harijans in factory canteens, or in cafés, for example. Most workers say their friends may be of any caste, and they make an explicit distinction between friendship, which is free, and the sphere where caste rules apply. ('As far as my family is concerned, I follow the rules; but friendship is different from the family.') Sometimes this is just the thing to say in public, and it turns out that all a man's close friends belong to castes of similar standing. The idea that Harijans are 'dirty' in their habits is sometimes a rationalization

---

[28] *Homo hierarchicus: the case system and its implications* (London, 1970).

Marriage

for keeping them apart as Harijans, sometimes a reason for distinguishing between Harijans whose homes are 'clean' (those who can be friends) and the rest (i.e. poor Harijans, who have no education and still work as unskilled labourers, sweepers etc.). Workers who spend a good deal of their time with lower-caste friends – and I met such men among their friends – may not be able to invite them home. I asked a man of middle caste whether he could invite his Harijan friends home for dinner: he hesitated, and said 'We go to their house.' (I doubt it.) It is only real conservatives who will say, as a young skilled worker did, that his friends are all of his own caste, his acquaintances of other castes, but he had no idea about Harijans. I believe some middle-class Harijans 'pass' for middle castes in the town, only partly deceiving their neighbours. Other Harijans and young radical Brahmans rebel openly against the restrictions on behaviour which affect them the most, and sometimes seek each other's company.

But the old pollution rules did not work mechanically, in every situation. Outside the house, especially in the fields and some religious cults, restrictions on touching, eating together and sex did not apply or were ignored. The tendency to define polluting situations narrowly is not new: it has gone further, partly as a matter of convenience in a new environment, partly because new ideals have altered the old unstable balance between hierarchy and equality. Caste difference survives as a simple segmentary division of society for some purposes; caste solidarity has its uses and some moral force; but there is not much left of hierarchy or structure.[29] Castes are 'separate but equal', and the only kind of separation between castes that really matters is endogamy.

Marriage

The old ambiguity about caste ranking, and about caste and subcaste boundaries, allowed families to adjust their marriage circles to changes in wealth and power (see footnote 5, p. 33). Without openly breaking caste rules, whole castes or subcastes could move up or down, and splinter groups could get themselves recognized as belonging to another caste: so a simple contrast between caste and ('modern') class is partly irrelevant. But there were limits, beyond which marriage was

---

[29] 'There is a shift from the caste system to individual castes ... Castes exist but, it would appear, the caste system has ceased to be.' D. F. Pocock, ' "Difference" in East Africa: a study of caste and religion in modern Indian society', *Southwestern Journal of Anthropology*, 13:4 (1957), 289–300 (p. 290).

plainly intercaste, and forbidden. These limits are sometimes crossed now, when marriages are *admitted* to be intermarriages. This happens because a weakening of caste solidarity allows families to put security, if not status, before everything else, and to arrange marriages with families having similar economic prospects; and because young men and women are increasingly taken with the idea, not just of choosing their own careers and life styles, but of marrying for love. Some are already in a position to meet, to talk, and to put this romantic ideal into practice. Love marriage is expected to be intercaste, and vice versa; in fact, however, many love marriages are in the caste, usually with relatives who visit the house often, and a very few parents arrange intercommunal marriages for their children (especially between Hindus and Christians).

The usual pattern is still one of arranged marriages within the subcaste. One man explained it like this:

In arranging a marriage, we find out about the other family's history and background by talking to their close relatives and friends. If we are satisfied, we try to establish close relations with them. People who marry out of caste can do as they please: but 'society' makes it hard for people born of mixed castes, and this would be a disgrace for our family. The very poor have bad habits, like drinking, gambling and wasting money. But, he added, 'nowadays everyone is equal . . . When we are in the factory, we are all one'; and he invites Harijan colleagues home to family festivals. Equality will come slowly.

No reference to the couple's wishes. But quite often the couple know each other, and the man or both of them suggest the marriage to their parents, who then arrange it.

A Brahman clerk said he and his Brahman wife both suggested marriage to their parents, but agreed beforehand not to go against their parents' wishes (see p. 94). It was 'not the biological urge' that brought them together. He disapproves of couples meeting at clubs in the factory, and of inter-marriage.

In other cases parents 'arrange' a marriage to avoid being faced with an accomplished fact, or the scandal of a love marriage. Some more opinions:

A Christian: 'Let them convert and get married' – one wants one's children to marry into good, respected well-off families. A Harijan: love marriage is bad, because the man will go to brothels and neglect his parents; but let people do as they please. A Brahman communist (who left his parents because he was in love, but that came to nothing) said that one day his family will marry him off – at least there will be no dowry. Young men of all castes repeat the proverb: there are only two 'castes' (or kinds) of people – male and female. A middle-aged man: now people who marry out may be boycotted by relatives, but this will not happen to the next generation – at least not if they are educated, e.g. if his son is a doctor. (Many people said this: if their children have more education, they can marry anyone.) A Harijan: intermarriage is 'scientifically good'. Another Harijan: intermarriages often do not last, especially when the partners are uneducated; if the husband has an accident, the couple's parents will not help. Though in one way intermarriage is good – if a low-caste man marries a Brahman girl, 'he may become clever too'. One slightly effeminate man did not want to marry, but said his family and community would force him into it. Another man had gone to the funeral of a friend, who had committed suicide just before his wedding date.

Only three men (in the case study sample of sixty-three presently married men) had married out of caste, but I know others who have, and everyone talks about cases. The opinions they expressed are tabulated in table 26. The tendency to tolerate love marriage, or at least to allow the couple some choice, is partly the effect of foreign models, and of Indian films and magazine stories: the Romeo and Juliet theme is immensely popular. And arranged marriage may be hard to reconcile with an individualistic career structure, where men and now some women expect, or want, to make their own lives. Not everyone can put family life and relations at work into separate compartments, with different rules and opportunities for choice.

Few young men and women get the chance to put this ideal of marriage by free choice into practice. It is hard to meet and talk to the other sex, except visitors who come to the house, though some do manage to meet at work or, for instance, in factory dramatic clubs.

TABLE 26. *Opinions about caste and intermarriage (case study sample)*

Strongly against caste, for marriage and everything	26%
Against caste, but not strongly or unambiguously	8
People should marry in their caste, otherwise caste does not matter: willing to eat with Harijans etc.	17
Intermarriage is all right, but one cannot hold out against family pressure	1
Intermarriage will come, but not yet	7
People should marry in their own religion: caste does not matter	5
More or less orthodox about caste	14
Strictly orthodox	3
No clear opinion	20

Then they are reluctant to hurt the feelings of their parents or older relatives, to cause scandal, or to damage their siblings' marriage prospects. Rather than force the issue, they will leave it to the next generation. When a couple do run away to get married, the families generally accept the situation at once, or perhaps a year later.

The argument is about marriage, not sexual freedom. Sexual morality is rigid and almost beyond question, even if an older generation had some discreet vices. The press gives lurid reports of western permissiveness, but the sexual revolution seems a long way off.

Two or three children are enough. Factory workers have taken the government's family planning message to heart: have no more children than you can afford to feed and educate. Some say they will stop (or have stopped) after the second, even if both are daughters. After the third, many take it for granted their wives will be sterilized, and the hospital staff try to persuade them to do so. Vasectomy does not seem popular, in spite of propaganda and incentives. Men use condoms, the only contraceptives that are cheap and easily available. Muslims and Catholics are said not to plan their families, but I am not sure this is true.

Have a small family and give them a good start, many parents say: the only thing one can leave them is education, not property, and the boys will make their own way in the world. It would be good if they became doctors, engineers or government officers, but at least they should do better than their fathers. One man said only Brahmans choose their sons' careers, and he seems to be right. Another said his sons should have enough education for toolroom work, not enough to make them unemployable; but he was unusual. Girls need enough education to marry educated men. But an educated woman's earning power now affects her marriage prospects: it is like a dowry.

The idea or possibility of choosing one's own personal life is not new. It was there in bhakti or devotional religion, where all castes might mingle in sectarian worship; in the ideal of disinterested friendship between men, which should have no trace of inequality and which often carries a great emotional charge; even in the romantic tradition of marriage by choice in the heroic days, or of Krisn'a's adulterous (therefore free, and higher) love of Raadhaa and the cowgirls.

But only the sannyaasi, the renouncer, could really choose his way of life, at the cost of all social and family ties. Bhakti was an optional

Marriage

extra for those who continued to play their social roles without attachment, an internal escape from social determinism.[30]

This tendency within Hinduism emphasizes the personal relation between an individual and his chosen god. For the Hindu majority, this is no longer something marginal to the prescribed religion of the caste society. Bhakti has become the centre of most people's religious thought and practice: it involves worship of personal rather than lineage or caste gods at home, private prayer and congregational worship in temples (with or without a Brahman priest), religious clubs and hymn-singing groups (bhajana), visits to gurus and svaamijiis, or an ideology of service to humanity expressed in religious language. The kinds of worship that are bound by caste and caste purity are becoming marginal instead. They are still necessary, but only in restricted situations: thus most castes still need a Brahman to perform weddings. Some sects, or politico-religious movements like the DMK, offer casteless alternatives even for weddings.

In chapter 6 I suggest that in thinking about caste, marriage, careers, politics and religion, these people now tend to place the individual at the centre of attention, the free agent as the bearer of value. The emphasis is new but not the idea. We should see the change not just as an import of foreign ideas, or a necessary consequence of industrialization, but as a new stage in an old dialectic in India between two models of man in society: a holistic, hierarchical model which was dominant; and a tradition of choice and equality, traditionally expressed in religious terms, which was marginal but is becoming dominant because more people find it relevant to their lives.

[30] 'An individual religion based upon choice is added on to the religion of the group.' (L. Dumont, 'World renunciation in Indian religions', *Contributions to Indian Sociology*, 4 (1960), 33–62 (p. 46); repr. in Dumont, *Religion/politics and history in India* (Paris and The Hague, 1970), p. 46.) In the bhakti sects, which make the sannyaasi's insights available to the 'man-in-the-world', Dumont notes, 'the sect appears as a religion for the individual superimposed upon common religion, even if this latter is relativized to the point at which Brahmanism is viewed simply as the order, or disorder, of the day-to-day world. The caste order continues to be respected, even if it is seen, in the light of sectarian truth, as a profane concern' (p. 60/repr. p. 58).

4

Some careers

This chapter is about individuals: some of the workers who gave up their evenings and Sundays to tell me their life stories, to answer questions and to ask about my work and country and opinions.[1] This kind of fieldwork is and ought to be an exchange of information, in which the fieldworker may have to answer almost as many questions as he asks. This is so particularly when one is under the obligations of a guest, as I was: sitting in my informant's house, introduced by his friends, drinking the coffee and eating the snacks his wife had made for me, and taking up his free time.

Much of my time was spent looking for people: getting introductions to potential informants (especially those who would fill gaps in my sample and make it more representative) and travelling all over the city to contact workers from my four factories, whose addresses I had collected at casual meetings around the factory or in the company of friends; and then going from one address to another, hoping to find someone in at a time when it was convenient for him to talk to me, making appointments for further visits, and getting into conversation with local people who were curious about my work – often workers who had seen me around their factory. I used no technical aids like tape recorders or cameras, but preferred to travel light, carrying only a pen and paper in my pocket, to summarize interviews and sometimes to take down important passages verbatim.

The use of case studies

There are special problems in using case studies of this kind to support general conclusions. I have tried to combine the advantages of two extreme approaches. One is pure autobiography, with little or no sociological comment, and not related systematically to the informant's observed actions or to external facts: the result can be a most vivid picture, a personal document or imaginative reconstruction

[1] A few workers described here are not in the case study sample of 104 workers.

of the world as it looks from a certain point of view.[2] The other is the questionnaire method, breaking down the informant's statement into easily quantified bits of information (e.g. answers to standardized questions about his life history, economic circumstances, attitudes etc.).

To communicate unique personal experiences means classifying them and generalizing about them. This can be done without fragmenting the individual accounts or distorting their meaning. This chapter contains commented summaries of some of the case studies, grouped for convenience to represent distinctive types of workers.

For these people, how many ways are there of organizing their social experience into an intelligible whole, and how do these ways correspond to the observed 'facts' of the situation?

Clearly, as many ways as there are people. But to point up significant similarities and differences between individual accounts, one can distinguish types of factory worker, each type have a distinctive life experience and ways of interpreting that experience – if not a fully worked-out ideology, at least a characteristic *argument*, a public face having some relation to action.

We must assume that people act on beliefs (about facts and values): or that an action can be explained only to the extent that it can be seen as the outcome of identifiable ends and beliefs ('the logic of the situation'). Of course this assumption is sometimes wrong: some actions are irrational and cannot be explained at all. But beliefs are not isolated, private things. They are organized for public presentation in arguments or ideologies, with some degree of consistency. Clearly ideologies do not directly determine actions and cannot be inferred from actions as beliefs sometimes can. They have to be reconstructed from what people say as well as what they do. Since arguments are public things and develop through experience and social interaction, changes and growth in arguments can be related to the points of decision or crisis (in the life of an individual or a group) when ideas crystallize, and when the implicit logic of actions has to be made explicit and defended.

This does not mean that an ideology follows necessarily from a particular material or social situation. Clearly there is a connexion: interests give people motives to see the world in one way rather than another, and to fit new facts into a system which is already partly closed. But what sort of connexion this is (between interests and ideas)

[2] e.g. Oscar Lewis, *The children of Sánchez* (Harmondsworth, 1964); E. Montejo, *The autobiography of a runaway slave* (Harmondsworth, 1970); or Ursula Sharma's study of an Indian family in England, *Rampal and his family* (London, 1971).

is an open question, to be found out in each case. To say that people always have alternatives does not mean that one cannot understand why they choose as they do. So it is sometimes possible to see by what process of thought workers from similar backgrounds, with the same material interests, can arrive at sharply opposed ideological positions, and vice versa. Thus each argument is to be analysed at two levels: in its own terms (as coherent or inconsistent, having a certain structure and making certain significant distinctions, and as a good or bad explanation of the facts it is meant to explain), and in relation to the situation of the person giving it (his interests, the pressures on him etc.). In sorting them into a number of types, I have concentrated on one aspect: workers' intentions for the future, seen in the light of their past.

The paternalists

To begin with an explicit ideology: a small group, which controls the union in one private factory, have an ideology of loyalty to a paternalistic management. I describe them first, not because they are typical, but because they are articulate and their strongly stated ideological position contrasts both with that of other union activists and with many workers' lack of interest in public issues; and because it suggests the extent and limits of continuity with the hierarchical interdependence of groups, which is the ideology of dominant groups in traditional Hindu society.

These 'paternalists' (or 'filialists'?) are clerical, skilled or semi-skilled workers. The leaders are mostly Brahmans or Harijans – a pattern of alliance between top and bottom castes which seems to be emerging in politics as well in some places. They are very religious, mostly reformist Hindus, with an ambiguous ideal of human equality: the rich should work for the poor, the middle classes should devote themselves to social work, and social differences will gradually become less. The Harijans among them are more unequivocally against caste. Their supporters include some Christians and Muslims.

During my fieldwork this group won control of the union's executive committee and all its offices, ousting a more loosely organized group they regarded (wrongly) as being communistic, and of doubtful morals. The election was fought on a party list system: but these two parties in the union are not obviously connected with political parties outside. This union belongs to no federation and supports no party; some but not all the new leaders support the Jan Sangh, a right-wing nationalist party which appeals specially to Hindu revivalists but has tried to broaden its base by projecting a more modern and secular image.

These men were involved in starting a religious association with ill-defined aims: generally to promote study of Swami Vivekananda's work, to get visiting lecturers on religious subjects, and perhaps to give free tuition in school subjects to poor children (though this seemed little more than a pious hope). While I was there they got no further than an inaugural ceremony for the association, held one Sunday in a modern temple. Union leaders made speeches, a visiting Svaamijii (religious ascetic) preached, and the Harijan president of the union presented a gold-edged shawl to the firm's Brahman Managing Director (a modern variation on traditional ways of turning worldly success into status with a religious sanction – but the Brahman was formerly the giver of status!).

With financial help from the management, the association published a 'souvenir' booklet with articles in three languages, written by members for the occasion and dedicated to 'our beloved Managing Director'. Most of the articles in it were commented summaries of Vivekananda's work, emphasizing obedience, achieving strength through the 'centralization of wills', devotion to work without thought of reward, social service, religion as a way of life rather than a system of ritual, and national self-reliance:

> He who knows how to obey knows how to command. Learn obedience first. We want organization. Organization is power, and the secret of that is obedience. (Vivekananda)

> The rich should help the poor and an attitude of trusteeship [be] developed towards wealth... The worker should dedicate his service to the master who in turn should protect him with tender care and love... There should thus take place a harmonious blending of the sacred and secular, the temple and the factory, the pooja [worship] and the production. (From an article in English, 'Do we need religion?')

> Starting his career as an ordinary worker, by his tireless work and courage [the Managing Director] has built up one of the greatest factories in India... He is not merely a task master. His paternal attitude, his loving nature and his nobility towards his employees have all made him a popular figure.
>
> (The union vice-president)

Clearly much of this is aimed at the management. It contrasts sharply with the tone of confrontation which militants take in their public statements, even if in practice the 'paternalists' can drive just as hard a bargain with the management. Thus, soon after taking office, their leaders presented the management with a list of demands for better pay, allowances and conditions, very like the demands of the previous leadership. The minutes of meetings where these were discussed with the general manager and administrative officer show that the union representatives made repeated comparisons with 'the factory next door' – one with a communist union; and the presence of an alternative, militant leadership waiting to take over must have strengthened the 'paternalists' hand. Within a few weeks they won a substantial rise in workers' allowances and payments for long service.

In conversation the 'paternalist' leaders – and not only those of middle-class origin – defend an organic, conflict-free ideal of society, with some individual mobility in a justified hierarchy.

Naagaraajan, a Brahman steno-typist of about 25,[3] is an official in the union and the religious association. He is a teacher's son from Tamil Nadu. After getting his SSLC (Senior School Leaving Certificate) he took a typing examination and got a job in Bangalore, which he left after fifteen months because his present factory has better prospects. He expects to stay in the same job for life, because he likes the work, the people he works with and 'our beloved Managing Director', and the pay is good. He visits his family twice a year: they will probably marry him to a working girl, who can continue to earn after their marriage. He would not mind marrying outside the caste (i.e. for love) but this would injure his family's reputation. Anyway he meets no girls. (Most young men now say they would be ready to marry out of caste, or would like to: it is a commonplace. Although one must allow for those who tell a foreigner what they think he wants to hear, this man – like many others – evidently meant what he said.) He and two friends began to discuss caste among themselves: they agreed that the very idea of membership in a caste would probably go in the end, 'automatically, because the present situation is like that': people see foreign films and act like foreigners.

Anyway, all castes are 'equal': in fact Naagaraajan wrote an article in the 'souvenir' paraphrasing Vivekananda's opinions on spiritual equality: 'We are all human beings, but are we all equal? Certainly not, who says we are equal? Only the lunatic. . . Because we have more or less powers, more or less brain, more or less physical strength, it must make a difference between us. Yet we know that the doctrine of equality appeals to our hearts. We are all human beings. . . Unity in variety is the plan of the universe', and so on. I asked him what he meant by equality: he said that in practice it means the rich should help the poor – build schools, teach, provide free meals for poor

[3] In most cases I give approximate ages only, to conceal informants' identities.

children – and 'automatically' the country will improve, class differences will be reduced – though they can never disappear.

To find out the limits of obedience owed to a superior, I asked Naagaraajan to comment on a quotation from Vivekananda in the 'souvenir': 'Always learn first to be a servant, and then you will be fit to be a master. If your superiors order you to throw yourself into a river and catch a crocodile, you must obey, and then reason with him. Even if the order be wrong, first obey, and then contradict it.' Perhaps you should put off complying with the order until you have finished the job in hand (he said), and meanwhile your superior might see reason. But if he does not, your first duty is to obey. However, you should not obey an immoral order. Someone is your superior because of his work, knowledge or service.

In Naagaraajan's opinion, the union is there to promote the interests of the 'working class': this really means factory employees, not the very poor, with whom he has no contact. The previous union leaders were communistic, i.e. 'very rough and tough' (he said in English) with the management: his own party, which was more conciliatory, had already had some success in its first negotiations for higher allowances for workers, and expected more concessions.

Most of these are stock opinions, sincerely held, but only produced in answer to my leading questions, and echoed (with minor differences) by the informant's Brahman friends. I think their union work is disinterested. They are content with their lot, having a safe job, prospects of promotion, and a safe place in the family and caste network. Their concern for the poor, and for what they see as injustices in Indian society, is genuine, but theoretical: it is all the more important to them to keep up their contacts with Harijan colleagues of similar opinions.

Their religion is an activist, moralizing development from the tradition of devotional sects, and there is some blurring of the boundary between spiritual equality (always admitted in this kind of devotional religion) and social equality. Nationalism (especially the Jan Sangh's semi-religious nationalism) partly replaces caste pride.

Consider the structure of this argument. Naagaraajan's 'job' is almost the same as his 'career'. It is part of a system of relations in a justified organic hierarchy of different jobs, all of which are necessary, rather than a hierarchy of *classes*. Since all the jobs are interdependent, there are no sharp class or other divisions, e.g. between those who serve and are served. This is a restatement, in modern functional terms, of the traditional ideology of the interdependence of specialized ranked caste groups. But caste divisions are/ought to be no longer relevant to this new economic and social structure: in particular, the historic injustice done to Harijans must be put right. As for the mass of the very poor, casual labourers etc., it is difficult to fit them into the structure. Naagaraajan has little contact with them anyway; he expects/hopes that social work and benevolence will bring these people into the same organic unity of a modern economy in time.

But his career is not quite his whole life. His family relationships belong to another system: he will/should marry within the caste and keep up his ties with his family (living in another state). In time, probably, caste endogamy will (therefore: should) wither away under the influence of foreign models.

Notice that in this account 'will' often equals 'should'. It is as if there is a temporary unfortunate gap between 'is' and 'ought', which are thought to coincide more or less in traditional Hindu society (barring anomalies like the injustice to Untouchables); tend to coincide inside the pale of an organic unity existing now (like the factory Naagaraajan works in); and will coincide in a future when industrialization and social work will have brought the poor into the same kind of benevolent organization. It is normal for 'is' and 'ought' to coincide. Our duty, according to Naagaraajan, is to resolve the contradictions in the present state of affairs which prevent this identity from being realized.

Aar·umugam, president of the union and of the religious association, is a Harijan semi-skilled worker of about 30. After dropping out of high school he took a Tamil correspondence course in homeopathy, but never practised except as a hobby. He was unemployed for a year. His father, a club servant, approached the manager of another factory at the club and got the son a job. A year later Aar·umugam's present factory was being set up, and his father approached an engineer at the club and got the son a better job. Aar·umugam says the job is not varied, but working conditions are good and the management is fair. He will stay for life. He lives with his wife and two small children in a two-room tenement, in a mixed-caste industrial suburb. His friends are of many castes: they are strongly anticaste and some have married girls of different castes, for love. He will only arrange his own children's marriages if they ask him to. He is a devout Hindu and a Jan Sangh supporter.

Aar·umugam and six others founded the union to demand higher wages. They organised the first strike when a supervisor injured a worker; and they opposed the laying off of 155 girl workers. The Managing Director was not to blame, and things have improved greatly since then. For several years the rival party, who were 'communistic' and make trouble about petty grievances, had controlled the union; but his own party had just regained control. The communists, in his view, were out to make trouble between classes, to destroy India's wealth, and to put the man living in a big house into a hut instead of vice versa. The first strike had been enough to bring the management to their senses; and (he said) he and his colleagues had got more concessions from the management in the month since the election than their opponents had been able to get in a long time.

Aar'umugam's job will be his career because no alternative is likely to be as good. His career coincides with his lifetime more closely than for Naagaraajan, since industrial work is his one chance to move into a new kind of society, where caste and class lines are less rigid than they were for his father's generation. The new class system is less rigid (from his point of view). The management's ideology of achievement, promotion on merit etc. is not entirely inconsistent with his experience: once inside the factory, he *has* risen partly by his own efforts. The Managing Director may be middle class and high caste, but he figures as a self-made man. The really important divisions are still between castes, not classes, especially between Harijans and the rest: but Aar'umugam thinks that industrialization, nationalism, religion and social work will eliminate these ancient differences.

Janardan, another Harijan union official, is a skilled machine setter in the top salary quartile,[4] about 30 years old. His father and grandfather were soldiers. After dropping out of high school he was selected for eighteen months' free training, with a small stipend, at a government Industrial Training Institute. His father, now retired from the army, was working as cook to an engineer who found Janardan a job in this factory. Now Janardan is in charge of several automatic machines, which work 'like magic'. He checks and repairs worn-out parts, sometimes making new components from drawings. The work is interesting because new problems arise all the time. He may move to another job, to get experience on other machines: he applied for and was offered two other jobs, but turned them down because one was in Madras, which is too hot for him, and the other paid badly. He has also thought of starting a small workshop with one or two employees, to make machine parts, but he does not know where to find capital.

Janardan was a founder of the union, because the management treated the workers very badly: the fault was not with the Managing Director but with some of his subordinates. Now the workers have a voice, and the differences between workers and officers are fewer. His party tells workers the truth about negotiations with the management, but their opponents lied, and some drank and were often absent from work.

He lives with his parents in a fairly large rented house in a mixed-caste area. He would like his son to study and to become an engineer or doctor. He has never had any bad experiences because of his low caste. Caste itself will

---

[4] Salary comparisons between factories are difficult because gross salary includes large allowances, which vary from factory to factory (see ch. 2). Private factories generally pay rather more than the public sector. A rough way to compare the economic condition of workers in the same factory is to divide the basic salary range into quartiles: thus equal numbers of workers are in the top, second, third and bottom quartiles.

probably continue, Janardan thinks, though people of different castes are close friends. There have been three or four love marriages between men and women working in his department, and 'love marriage is always in different castes'. The courting couples go to cinemas and parks together. He does not like love marriage, because some men who marry for love neglect their parents and go to brothels: of course others are free to do as they like. Though not a firm supporter of the Jan Sangh, he voted for the party because the ruling Congress Party was associated with the atheistic DMK party, which had just organized a shocking procession with images of naked gods in a town in Tamil Nadu (the Jan Sangh had made capital out of this incident in the election campaign). Janardan is indignant that the income tax threshold has been lowered, so that ordinary workers like him now have to pay the tax – about 1 per cent of his salary.

Sriinivaas, a Brahman steno-typist, is a village landlord's son of about 35. He failed to complete his B.Sc., studied shorthand and typing, and had four jobs in Bangalore with intervening periods of unemployment. Once he moved to a better-paid job, but left it because he was in a 'master and servant' relationship with a superior of his own subcaste, who was jealous and tried to keep him down. He is proud that he never used recommendations to get a job, only 'merit'.

He had just come back from a six-week course in punched-card accountancy and he hoped this would eventually bring him promotion. Since the management paid for the course he thinks it only fair to stay at least three more years, and he will probably stay for life: now he is over 30 and must settle down, and employers would have no confidence in a man who keeps changing jobs. He is active in the factory's Fine Arts Club, which puts on plays and entertainments with a management subsidy.

Sriinivaas lives in an apartment in a middle-class suburb, with his widowed mother, his wife and child: even before his father's death his brothers left the joint household, one by one, because their wives quarrelled – especially over differences in their husband's salaries (but quarrels between women are traditionally the man's excuse for leaving a joint family) – and also because they could not afford a big enough house. I suggested it would be cheaper for them to share a large house than to rent smaller separate ones. Yes, he replied, but there would not be enough privacy for each husband and wife – it is all right for the children, who share bedrooms anyway.

His wife is a typist. (I think she has gone back to work since her daughter was born four months ago.) She is of the same caste, and he has known her since childhood. They agreed to marry, or to 'part as friends' if their parents objected; in fact the parents gave their consent, so to that extent 'it is an arranged marriage'. It was not 'the biological urge' which brought them together. He disapproves of intercaste marriage, because he wants to live in a religious way – others can do as they will, but Brahmans have special duties, and intermarriage would hurt their parents. Some couples first meet in the factory.

Militant unionists

Family planning is necessary, Sriinivaas thinks, but publicity for contraceptives is bad, because it makes young people think they can satisfy their 'biological urges' without children, as in western countries where divorce is common. Contraceptives should be available only to 'legally wedded couples who have society's permission to sleep together': yet the government hands out condoms even to bachelors with their pay packets.

The division of society into castes will continue Sriinivaas says, because the present generation sees that the old ways are best and is going back to them. He would eat with a Harijan, but not at home because of his mother; and (he says) his friends are of other castes. The gap between rich and poor should be reduced, but not by making the rich poorer. People should be more dedicated to their jobs, and should have more opportunities to accumulate capital. The outgoing union officials were too ready to strike or disturb production: there should be better understanding with the management.

Generally this group are socially and politically conservative, moralistic and puritanical, and not very ambitious. They would hold the management to the fulfilment of paternalistic obligations. But their leaders are quite ready to escalate their demands and the management, for the time being, is willing to make concessions: by raising 'allowances' rather than the basic wage, which might commit the management to bigger rises in future and could also cause more unrest among workers at other Bangalore factories and ill-feeling between managements. The market for the factory's products is protected by import controls and the lack of strong competitors, labour trouble is expensive, and many factory officers come from the same kind of background as their skilled workers and share the same assumptions. Other men in this group of workers say there should be no gap between capitalists and workers; workers should share in decision making; and friendly negotiation with the good men at the top will achieve a lot.

Militant unionists

Another clear ideology is that of the militant unionists, dedicated to the interests of the 'working class'. But who are the working class? People like themselves, in steady factory employment. Of course, they agree, casual labourers and workers in small workshops are worse paid and much less secure, and there is some difficulty in fitting them into the picture. When pressed, the militants admit the working class is a middle class: when speaking English (which they often do) they use 'working class' and 'middle class' almost interchangeably. Many but not all of this group support the Communist Party of

India (CPI) and its affiliated unions (see p. 66). The party's power base is in the organized industrial sector. It is exposed to attack from the left by groups like the Communist Party of India (Marxist) (CPI(M) or CPM), which have similar middle-class graduate leadership but which aim to build up a following in the unorganized sector. This is difficult to achieve: a CPI(M)-led union of restaurant and café workers declined when it became clear that it had no real bargaining power, and a pavement vendors' union lacks any clear function. So even would-be militant parties have to fall back on roughly the same industrial base as the CPI.

Although the two big federations (the communist AITUC and the pro-Congress INTUC) support parties, it is a mistake to see Indian unions as 'manipulated' by politicians: the manipulation is often in the other direction. A strong factory union can put pressure on politicians, and the federations seem to have little power to impose a common line on member unions.

This does not mean that labour militancy is explained by simple self-interest. The militants and some of their supporters are aware of the contradictions between their idealistic vision of society as it ought to be (and will be in the future) and their personal interests as members of a middle class; and some of them make real personal sacrifices.

Thomas is a middle-aged (in his fifties) Catholic skilled worker, an AITUC (communist) union official and a CPI member. The son of a small farmer, he worked in stores and restaurants, spent several years as a soldier, and then spent a year looking for work. One of his many applications for factory work succeeded. He could only get an unskilled job, because of his lack of education, but he soon transferred to a more skilled job inside the factory. He is well paid but finds it hard to support his many small children – he and his son, an electrician, have to support a household of eleven people. They own their house, and rent out part of it. He will stay in this factory until he retires; he has no idea what his children will do.

Thomas never thought about politics until he got involved in a bitter struggle between two unions at his factory: a Congress union became the recognized union, and the communist union's activities were restricted by the management. Communism was a Pauline conversation for him: his union's outside leader approached him personally and convinced him of its truth, so that he gave up his prospects of promotion, stopped going to Mass (unlike his family) and dedicated himself to union work. He wants socialism, which means freedom and rights for workers. The CPI is right to go 'step by step'; the CPI(M) says 'Go and attack those people immediately', which is impossible. He says Bangalore workers are difficult to organize, because they divide up on communal lines – union officials of the powerful

Okkaliga caste, for example, rely on Okkaliga support; members of the same language group hang together. (I believe this is more true of his own factory than of some others.) Thus the working class is held back.

Thomas spends his free time on union work. The management will not recognize his union or acknowledge its demands (which are for more pay, and especially for redress of individual grievances, e.g. reinstatement of employees sacked after a strike and riot). So his union makes its influence felt, and tries to recruit support, by putting its members into key positions on the many committees set up by the management of this public sector factory: a subsidized housing scheme committee, a Death Relief Fund, a co-operative and several others. Since they have run these committees efficiently and used the funds wisely, they are often (not always) re-elected to run them. Thomas himself has served on at least two committees.

His career (as he tells it) is made up of unrelated jobs, most of which he got by luck, and which form no logical progression. Going beyond what he said, this is how I reconstruct his argument: Some people are not lucky enough to have factory jobs, but their class situation is essentially the same as that of the factory workers. They have no control over their lives: the controlling class includes public sector management as much as (or almost as much as) private capitalists. Class conflict is concealed by communal jealousies, which the ruling classes encourage. Just as one's career is made up of an almost unrelated series of jobs, there is an almost accidental relationship between one's career and one's lifetime, which gets meaning and value to the extent that one identifies with the struggle and liberation of the working class – i.e. everyone who does not have real control over his life. Thomas is optimistic but does not seem certain about the success of this struggle, unlike others who are buoyed up by the marxist doctrine of historical inevitability.

A young Brahman semi-skilled worker, who has held office in the communist union in another factory, is the son of a village landlord who also runs a petrol station and has some other business. He hopes to complete his interrupted commerce degree: then he will go and farm his share of the family land. Agriculture is 'a free life'. Actually, he says, 'I don't like to have this land': he will give it to the farm labourers, work and live with them, and educate them politically. I think he sincerely intends now, at 23, to do this: we shall see.

A young friend of his, whose father has a small business, says all private property should be nationalized and redistributed, and he sees that his own class will lose. But, he says, he is used to living well and cannot afford to do so on factory pay when he marries (which he did a few months later): so he must 'jump into business' while keeping his revolutionary ideals.

These men are quite open about the conflict between their ideals and their situation. Not all are as young as these two.

A different case is that of a Harijan converted to Catholicism, who used to support the (all-Harijan) Republican Party until the outside leader of his

Some careers

union selected him for conversion to communism. Now he sees the Republican Party is interested in nothing but caste, but the class struggle is the thing. He lives in the factory township; but since he feels his work for the un-recognized union may endanger his job, he is buying a small house elsewhere in the city.

Another Catholic in the same factory comes from a poor village. He found it hard to get a job because the papers which advertise jobs do not come to his village, but a factory officer on leave met him and recommended his case. He is proud of his efficiency as a fitter, but he wants a clerical job because there is the same pay for 'horses and asses' and he might as well have a job where he keeps his clothes clean and is not exhausted at the end of the day. People should be rewarded according to their work; also (he said when challenged) according to their needs: a stonebreaker does not need brains, but should still have a better deal. Another man in the same union complains that all the 'plums' in the factory – such as foreign training – go to men recommended by the Congress union.

A career in the union or in politics

Another group (overlapping the previous one) use the union or politics as an alternative career ladder. Some are in it for what they can get: better prospects inside the factory, the chance of a political career outside, or the bribes which officials in *some* unions are alleged to take to find people jobs and so on. Others are certainly sincere, idealistic and uncorrupt.

One graduate, after three office jobs, became an apprentice in a public sector factory. He worked there as a technician, thought of taking a higher quali-fication, but then went into union work at a time when the union was at a very low ebb, with embezzlement of funds and other abuses, and built it up. He sees this as a 'logical development' after the social work he had done in voluntary associations as a student and afterwards. Once in the union, he 'never looked back': he helped to make it a showpiece of a union which was both conciliatory and tough, and which has kept out of all political federa-tions.

He says 'I haven't cultivated myself for a better job', and his future is un-decided. He rose to the lowest category of factory 'officers', who have minor privileges (officers do not 'clock in', for example). Now he spends most of his time on union affairs, and the management tacitly accept this. He advises unions in newly established factories, and has gone into local politics.

He says that there is built-in security in the public sector, but rather lower wages and fewer opportunities for advancement than in the private sector. This is not fair. The government should ensure, not only that indi-vidual workers can get ahead faster, but that the more efficient, well-managed factories are not held back for the sake or parity of wages in the public sector; but all public sector workers should have at least a 'need-based minimum wage'. In the long run there will and should be more social equality. It is true that industrial workers now tend to form a self-perpetuating middle class, and have a vested interest in keeping what they have achieved. This is a 'natural consequence' of industrialization, and will continue until faster industrialization creates a need for more workers. Any factory needs men to do 'what used to be called menial work' – casual labourers, sweepers and so on – but these people's sons are now going into skilled trades. Educated men also take labouring jobs in a factory, in the hope of transferring to a better job when one is advertised internally; though only people belonging to certain castes will take work as sweepers or gardeners. Since the middle classes now find great difficulty in finding jobs, in some ways they are worse off than the poor, who are willing to take any kind of job and usually find something in the end.

An ambitious, educated and fairly idealistic lieutenants of this graduate – the son of a police officer – could not afford to continue his studies, and took a clerical job in the factory. He was 'sober minded' for eighteen months. Then he thought he was getting 'mentally old' and should 'jump into some public service' and stand for union office. None of the other white-collar workers would, being a timid lot. The management have given him an easy job (three hours of work a day) so that he can spend most of his time on union work. His ideology is one of hard work, political honesty (he thinks the country's troubles are caused by corrupt politicians, especially older ones) and middle-class respectability (he would like to marry for love, with caste no bar, but not a factory girl, because they speak too freely and do not come from respectable families). He may go to Canada, where he has relatives, to work for some years; or stay in this factory doing union work and exploring possibilities; or, if he can get capital, start an agency supplying raw materials for factories; or (his favourite plan) buy ten acres for a mechanized farm.

Another man does hardly any factory work since he became a Provident Fund Trustee. When his term of office is up, he hopes for a supervisory job: a 'group leader' (lower-level supervisor) need not work, he says, but just 'extract work' from others. Or he might go into politics; anyway he will not go back to an ordinary job. He too says the middle class are the hardest hit by unemployment, because they cannot take any job as labourers can. The government should help them – for example, by subsidizing private schools.

The young president of another union failed to get into college. After six months as an apprentice he was 'demoted' to unskilled worker for taking part in a strike, which is against the rules for apprentices: so he stopped looking for promotion and devoted all his energies to the union. He hopes to become a full-time outside union leader, like a young communist graduate whom he takes as his model, and who mediates between this militant union and the management. In this case he will have to join the party, which is the only party supporting the workers: he knows little about the party's ideas and policies outside the union field.

For a few middle-class workers, 'leadership' is an end in itself – the material rewards seem less important.

A meticulous and conservative young man of middle caste, the son of a railway clerk, stayed on after training as an instructor in his factory's training section. His main aim is to get into a situation with no one over him. ('My conscience [he said in English] doesn't permit me to work under somebody's pressure.') While he was job-hunting he supervised labour for building contractors, and acquired a taste for supervising others. Now 'there is not much pressure from the top: only two people are above me' (in his own section, presumably). He will stay in this factory for life. He concentrates on perfecting his knowledge of the trade and improving his position in his section. He does a little 'social work' ('Those who call on me to help with their family affairs, or any other transaction, I attend to their call') and might stand for some union office: but this would be expensive – you have to pay for printing handbills and take your supporters to cafés. ('Unless you show cash to them, people will not convass for you. . . . A sincere worker can't come up, unless he spends a little on the others.')

Idealistic, reforming, middle-class factory workers

Many workers fall into this group: men from a middle- or lower-middle-class family who feel secure in their jobs, expect some promotion, and share an ideology of moderate social reform, service to the nation, and sometimes the moral superiority of the public sector. They are the backbone of clubs, associations and unions, where they serve conscientiously without expecting high office.

Naaraayan·, a skilled worker of about 35, comes from a Mudaliaar (middle-to high-caste) family. His family had land in a village which grew into a town. His grandfather was a landlord, contractor and politician; his father, a retired minor civil servant, sold the land to two brothers and now lives with Naaraayan· in the factory township, together with Naaraayan·'s wife, his three children and his younger brother and sister, who works in the same factory. This sister's husband is a soldier, stationed in North India.

Naaraayan· got his job because a school friend's father applied on behalf of the two boys. When he was called for an interview, his father and teachers wanted him to complete his studies, but his friends said this was too good an opportunity to miss. In those days people did not think highly of factory work, but this has changed now. At one time he considered starting a small business supplying components to the same factory, since he knows the officers there, but he was advised against it. He might take another job if it were offered to him, but he has never applied for a job in his life. The security of a public sector job justifies the lower pay; besides, the public sector has a responsibility to 'support' more workers, and the profits go to the nation, not to individuals.

In his seventeen years' service he has done various jobs in the same department and his promotion has been steady but slow. He thinks he would get quicker promotion if the management could promote workers for efficiency rather than seniority, but as a loyal unionist he cannot oppose the management–union agreement on promotion by seniority only. The only way to bypass the procedure would be to gain admission to the factory's evening classes leading to a diploma in engineering, and then to get appointed as a technical assistant, but he is not thinking seriously of this at the moment.

Naaraayan˙ has sat on various union committees and does routine work for the union. He trained as a 'worker–teacher' under the Workers' Education scheme, sponsored jointly by the government and most unions, and expects to take short periods away from his usual work to give other workers courses in union organization, labour law etc. He seems to have no ambition for union office. He knows factory workers are a privileged middle class. (His definition of 'middle class' is anyone earning over Rs 500 a month – as he does, when overtime and bonuses are taken into account.) He looks to the success of the government's five-year plans to bring the same benefits to the unemployed and low-paid workers. He says his friends are of any caste. (I think this is true.) Scheduled Caste friends come to his house: 'If they are clean, I have no objection' – nowadays they keep their houses like other people, and their way of life (i.e. that of middle-class Harijans) can no longer be distinguished from that of other castes. It is no longer considered 'decent' to talk about caste (though he had a lot to say about language groups, especially Kannad'a resentment of Tamil workers like himself). One gets to know people's caste indirectly, by attending ceremonies in their family. But arranged marriages, within the caste, are much the best. Although a few workers in his factory marry for love, their lives are not satisfying, because there is no close bond between husband and wife: often they quarrel over trivial matters and the marriage breaks up. (At this point he checked himself and said my own case – of course – might be different!) Those whose marriage is arranged are happy, because arguments between the couple are settled by relatives.

Sundaram is a skilled Brahman worker of about 30. His grandfather was a village headman, who was forced by famine and drought to sell much of his land. Sundaram's father is a retired clerk and small landowner. Sundaram left school at 18 with SSLC, learned typing and shorthand, and hoped to take a commerce degree and become a clerk, or even a Lecturer in commerce. But since his family depended on him, he answered a newspaper advertisement for a technical job in this public sector factory: he says he had no recommendations from anyone. The work is skilled but often repetitive: sometimes he has to assemble prototypes from engineers' drawings, and he received a small reward (Rs 75) for suggesting a simpler and cheaper model of one type of equipment. He has taken some short technical courses in the factory, but thinks a diploma course would involve too much expense (and trouble?), even with aid from the factory. With his qualifications, he might become a supervisor or perhaps a technical assistant.

He lives with his wife and two daughters. He does not want a son (in spite of the traditional brahmanical emphasis on continuing the male line), since one should not have children unless they can be well educated and find employment: so he volunteered the information that he and his wife use 'family planning' (meaning contraceptives, or sterilization). They also live with his unmarried younger brother, for whom Sundaram found a job in the same factory four years ago; much of the brother's earnings goes to support their parents' household. He has to budget carefully to live within his income without taking loans ('the clever way in which I spend – that is the answer'): he has no luxuries; and when he manages to save anything, he puts it towards a new house he is building for his parents in their village. He expects to stay in the same factory for life.

Sundaram says his friends are of any caste, including Harijans, and that they can come to his house. He does not go to temples often: since reading Vivekananda and Ramakrishna, he tries to see God in every person. He is active in a drama group, whose members pay all the expenses of their own productions and give the takings to charity: to orphanages, for a poor girl's marriage, and to the Deaf Aid Society. They prefer 'social' to historical or mythological themes, partly because they save on costumes. One play showed that intercaste marriage need not lead to 'misunderstandings' if the couple are both educated; another showed the love of a capitalist's daughter for a poor boy, and how the difference in wealth came in the way of their love – the moral being that everyone is equally a human being and the human heart is very sensitive. The group also perform some comedies and musical entertainments.

Whenever the union needs volunteers, Sundaram offers himself. In a stay-in strike, he brought meals to the workers. He takes over some routine work when his (union) general council member goes on leave. He supports no party, but prefers the Jan Sangh because of their pride in nationality. Land reform should come about, he thinks, not by compulsion, but by voluntary sacrifice; compulsion would lead to calamities, and 'we will lose our own property'. A friend and neighbour he greatly admires is another factory worker, who is also a 'social worker': he is not only active in the drama group and a Telugu cultural association, but goes without being called when anyone is ill or short of money, whatever the person's caste or religion, and does what he can: thus he took fifteen days' leave to be with a poor worker whose leg was amputated in hospital.

No alternatives

But for many workers – especially unskilled ones without much education – there are no alternatives anyway and little chance of anything better than promotion by seniority. They need the union for help with specific grievances, like promotion.

Raamayya, a semi-skilled machine operator, is the son of a bangle-seller belonging to a middle caste whose traditional occupation this is. He is 28 but looks much older, and has been in his present job for nine years.

He was born in a village and left school at 9, to work as a labourer until his family moved to Bangalore when he was 14. He got a job as helper to a tractor driver in the suburbs and learned to drive the tractor himself. He also worked for six months in one factory, as a temporary labourer. Then he told an engineer he had a big family to support, and got a job in the stores. Five years later, he qualified more or less automatically for transfer to the machine shop, where he does a repetitive job and waits for his next promotion by seniority; but he does not expect to go far, because he has no SSLC.

Two years ago he married, for love and against his parent's wishes, a girl of the same caste whom he met at work. They soon separated, and he is waiting for a divorce. He says he is against intercaste marriage because the caste is against it: but his friends can be of any caste, and visit his house. He voted 'for Indira' because his friends did. He lives in an urban village with his parents and brothers, and says they live rather better than their neighbours.

His 21-year-old brother [Raamakrisn'a] worked for a year in a small welding shop. Then Raamayya and the welding shop owner (whose brother is a foreman in Raamayya's factory) got him a casual labourer's job in the factory. After a year his job was confirmed. He will stay in this factory all his life: in five years he hopes to transfer to a technical job.

A group of three labourers in a village near a factory:

Deevaraaj, 23, works in the stores. His family are of a peasant caste, and lived in a rural village where he kept a bullock cart. Since his father was dead, the whole family came to Bangalore when Deevaraaj's brother, a postman, was transferred. Deevaraaj worked as a building labourer, a plumber's mate and a mill worker. Then he got casual work with a builder working at the factory, and contacted someone who got him a regular job there. He would like to learn a skill but sees little chance of that because he has only a few years' education. He will stay, of course.

Muniappa, a 30-year-old Harijan, works with him in the stores. He is illiterate, and will stay for life. His father does casual farm labour; he thinks his children might become factory workers.

Paapann·a, a 28-year-old Harijan maintenance worker, is on the union's executive committee. He was working as a casual labourer (like his father, who is usually unemployed) when a government labour officer recommended him for a job in this private factory. He is illiterate and cannot go elsewhere, but he would like a chance to learn a new job in the factory. I asked him about his union work; he said he just collects subscriptions, sends up demands and does routine work in his department – he has no very clear ideas about it.

Raaju, whose father was an army officer, dropped out of college and spent several months applying for factory jobs. His present factory took him (like another man I met) so that he could play in the factory football team. He did a semi-skilled job for five years, then left to play for professional football clubs in Calcutta for five years. Football pays well but there is no security, and once a player is injured he is finished. So he applied for his old job again, and was taken back without difficulty – again because of his football. He dislikes the work – he wants a job in sports, perhaps as a coach, but cannot afford the training. He lives with his mother, who cannot afford to arrange a marriage for him. He is not interested in politics, the union or anything much except football.

Some have special reasons for staying:

Tyaagaraajan, whose family farmed land on the outskirts of Bangalore, left school at 16 and spent two years looking for a factory job. He worked as an unskilled helper in his present factory for two years, transferred to another department where he helped a skilled machine operator, and was recommended for a two-year apprenticeship in toolmaking. Six months before the end of the course he broke a leg at work; after ten months away from work, he came back and completed the course. (He was awaiting the result of the final test when I met him.) He expects the union will soon get him compensation for his broken leg. Now toolmakers are in demand; but he would hesitate to take a job elsewhere because, if his leg troubles him later, his present factory will feel bound to help him, as another firm would not.

Hopeless cases

A few men cling to a job which is getting too much for them. Their promotion is blocked, they are constantly getting into trouble with the management, they are metaphorically and sometimes literally accident-prone. I met them on what is perhaps the last lap of their factory career, before even the organized sector's built-in security runs out on them.

Anthony is a Catholic skilled worker, apparently of a Harijan family. His grandfather and father were policemen. Anthony spent five years in the Armed Reserve Police under the British, and took part in lathi charges on strikers and rioters. He liked police work but not the low pay, so after Independence he joined a small factory and studied turning and fitting at a small workshop in his spare time. With several workers from that factory, he came to his present factory when it was founded. He learned to operate various machines and became a skilled turner. He has had no promotion for eight years, though the foreman once recommended him. Now the foreman has no full-time work for him, but keeps him as a 'spare' to replace sick or absent workers and to train newcomers.

Factory a good place to work; why leave?

Since he had no increments and was not allowed to work properly on the machines, Anthony got fed up and (he says) very inefficient. The manager called him and gave him a 'show-cause notice', warning him to improve his efficiency or lose his job. Then, six months ago, he injured his hand and was off work for two months. He got only the Employees' State Insurance benefit, about two-thirds of his regular wages. He was put on light work. His mother died, and he fell into a deep depression.

Five of his seven children are at a convent school, and he finds it hard to manage. He would like another job but has no chance because of his age and poor education. He used to play football, make up Tamil plays for a drama group, and play the guitar, but depression and his injured hand now prevent him from doing these things, and he does not know how to spend the rest of his life: 'Now it has become dust', he said, holding out his guitar to me. I tried to cheer him up, saying everyone has bad periods and things will look different in a few months. But with his present attitude to life and work, what chance has he of keeping even his present job? His relatives also have large families, and some are unemployed or in casual work. To what depths of poverty and helplessness can he sink? Yet he is more fortunate than many.

Factory a good place to work; why leave?

At the other extreme, some sing the praises of the factory they work in, though they have no special attachment to a paternalistic setup or an ideal of obedience and respect. The conditions are much better than in other jobs they know of, there are perquisites, and the atmosphere at work is friendly. Sometimes the economic advantages are almost taken for granted, and only the emotional ones are stressed: their model factory is a system of warm personal relations between generous people, with manufacturing almost as a by-product.

Goovindappa, a group leader, was recommended for his job by a friend, whose father was a state minister. He says: 'This is my first and last factory.' He regards himself as a guide to workers under him, and values friendly relations partly but not only as a means of control. ('I am not strict: I enjoy myself with them socially and joke with them; therefore they are all obedient to me.') We must manage with what we get, he says; and he would not leave this factory for a thousand rupees a month. 'From top to bottom we are all as brothers and friends. No, I can't leave these people. I will give you an example: this is my family...' – they have lived together since childhood and cannot leave. And he means it. He lives in a rather conservative, warm-hearted family of middle-caste and peasant origins: very idyllic. He says he wants socialism, which means 'no difference between high and low – the same as the factory... I want to be friendly with everyone – the same in politics.' The reason why workers in smaller workshops have a bad deal is that the owners are selfish.

Conditions will improve when small factories merge to form large ones, because if one owner is stingy, another has a 'free heart' or is a 'socialist'.

Venkat araaman, a skilled worker of middle caste, is on the executive committee of the 'paternalist' union, of which his Harijan friend and neighbour Aar umugam (pp. 92–3) is president. His grandfather was a farmer, his father an office peon or messenger. He left school at 18, without SSLC, and spent five years in two small engineering works before a relative put in a word for him with an engineer working in his present factory. He became an assistant turner, and then trained for a different trade. The work is hard but not dull. He will stay in the same job because this is a very good factory, with good pay and facilities, free medical treatment and uniform, and subsidized meals: but the pay should be still higher and the management should provide housing. He is interested in the union because of the 'good president [his friend], good employees, good management'. He is also on the committee of the factory's religious association; but he does nôt share the explicitly paternalist ideal of the other leaders of this association and the union.

He lives with his wife (who works in the same factory), their baby daughter, his unemployed elder brother and the brother's wife and seven children. They live as a joint family, and he gives his pay packet to his elder brother and asks for money when he needs it. They keep a cycle hire and repair shop, which employs three labourers and makes a small profit.

He met his wife in the factory and proposed to her there: unlike some others, he had no chance to take her out walking or to the cinema until they married. Her family belong to a higher caste and opposed the marriage, but are reconciled to it. There should be no rich or poor and no caste distinctions, Venkat araaman says: Harijan friends can come into his house. (This is true.)

Factory owner's kith and kin

A group in one factory were recruited when they left school by one of the partners who own the factory, and at least a third of them are of the partner's caste. Several are in supervisory jobs, not necessarily because they get preference but because many of them have been in the factory since it opened.

Once in Bangalore, few of them leave. Some say they could not, even if they had a better offer, because the partner brought them and if they left he could make trouble for their families, refuse to employ their younger brothers and so on. (I do not know if this is true.) Not that they see anything of the partner in Bangalore or feel any personal loyalty towards him: he does not seem to expect it – just that they keep their side of the implied bargain.

Narasappa, a group leader, belongs to the partner's caste. His parents belonged to a co-operative; and the partner, being the 'big man' of that town, helped members' children with their school expenses. Yet Narasappa had to leave school at 17, without SSLC, because of financial difficulties. (This may or may not mean he failed the examination.) Anyway the partner interviewed all SSLC candidates from the town, and asked Narasappa why he did not want to study any more. Narasappa said that all his family depended on him, so the partner gave him a job in the new factory. His father wanted him to study for a B.A., saying he would find the money somehow; but now, when Narasappa's father sees his salary, he thinks Narasappa is a big man and very lucky. The partner helps everyone from his own town, but naturally gives preference to his own caste, most of whom are poor.

Narasappa's first job was to unload and set up the machinery: hard, unskilled work, and so dirty that in the evening you could not sit next to someone on a city bus. Eighteen months later he became a machine operator, and a supervisor last year. He has worked different machines in the factory and earned several awards for suggestions. He said a certain machine could be made to do four men's work in one operation; the foreign engineer said this was impossible but Narasappa was welcome to try. In a week he solved the problem, and the workers doing that job were moved to another section – there is plenty of other work to be done in the factory, he says. He is quite well paid, and he could not leave because all his family depend on the partner. He lives with his wife and three children, and sends money back to his parents' family. People should keep up the old custom of marrying inside the caste, he says; but his friends may be of any caste (as I know his friends are). He spends his spare time in acting and sports.

Raajendra, another group leader of the same caste, was called to the partner's house when he passed SSLC and given a job in the new factory. He says the partner, and the partner's brother, have sixteen firms in two states, all run from one head office in their small town. Raajendra's younger brother worked in this office as a clerk, and recently transferred to this factory because he was more interested in technical work (anyway the pay and prospects were better). Very recently Raajendra's wife's brother came to work in the factory as a casual labourer. They all live together.

Kumaarasvaami, a semi-skilled worker belonging to another caste, comes from a village near the partner's home town. He failed SSLC and left school at 16. A doctor recommended him to the partner; and after six months in one of the partner's workshops he came to Bangalore as an unskilled worker in the new factory. Three years later he became a machine operator, and has been on the same machine for seven years. The work is hard and very monotonous, and he is bitter because he has had no promotion: the only way to get promotion, he says, is to do what the supervisor says, never answering back and asking no questions even when the supervisor is wrong. He sees no chance of getting another job, because he has no influential contacts. Other workers from the partner's home town tend to go back there if they leave the factory. (He did not suggest the partner had any sanction

Some careers

to prevent their leaving.) Every week Kumaarasvaami goes to an aashram (religious institution) where the devotees sing hymns and a Svaamijii answers questions. For Kumaarasvaami the important questions are about everyday practical problems. When he asked the Svaamijii how his younger brother could get a job, the Svaamijii gave them sacred ash and told them to pray; and six months later the brother found a job in the same factory.

An ideology of personal achievement

A very different group see chances of advancement through their own efforts, and have an ideology of personal achievement. These are the 'achievement-oriented' types D. C. McClelland thinks so strategically important to economic development.[5] They say they will make their own way in life, and they need no help from the union or anyone else. A man should receive a good wage for good work, or should go where he can find it: so they plan to raise money, through relatives or bank loans, to set up small workshops; or they prepare themselves for promotion to management jobs in the larger factories. Most come from comfortable middle-class backgrounds and expect to live well; their relatives are often in the kinds of executive or professional jobs these men aspire to. Most are young, presumably because those who succeed pass out of my universe of study and become managers or independent businessmen, while those who fail become disillusioned and pass into another group of factory workers (e.g. those who put security before everything). Many seem to be Christians, but the sample is small.

Michael, a Christian bachelor from Kerala, left school with SSLC to take a four-year course in toolmaking at a church institute. He went to Madras to look for work: here he stayed in a hotel with friends, but – he was careful to add – at his own expense (unlike many job-seekers who stay with friends or relatives). One firm offered him a job, but he turned it down because of the low pay and went to Bangalore. Within two weeks he had answered a newspaper advertisement and been appointed as a tool and die maker.

He and two other skilled men from the same factory are trying to raise money from their families, and a bank loan, to start their own toolroom making components for their present factory and other factories. They have in mind a particular site, with a shed. They seem likely to succeed.

Michael contrasts Hindu fatalism with the progressive mentality of Americans, who want material comforts and are prepared to work hard for

[5] See McClelland, 'The achievement motive in economic growth', and his 'The impulse to modernization' in M. Weiner (ed.), *Modernization* (New York, 1966), pp. 28–39. McClelland advocates a bizarre sort of psychological engineering to instil the 'need for achievement'.

them. If the Indian masses were really progressive they would not have remained poor. There has been little improvement since Independence – just strikes, communal riots and starvation, and the politicians are not entirely to blame for these things. If one man wants to work harder than others, Michael says, he must be given the opportunity to do so, and to get rich: though of course we should be patriotic and should not only think of ourselves.

One of Michael's partners, whose father farms forty acres in Kerala, dropped out of a pre-university course and entered the same church institute to study tool engineering. He turned down two factory jobs in other towns because of the low pay, and got into his present factory with the recommendation of the institute's principal. He says a socialist country can never improve, because equality in wealth is against human nature: however, the present gap between rich and poor is too big. India needs a strong government – perhaps a 'democratic-minded dictator'.

Yet another Christian toolmaker will be an ordinary worker for five years and then look for a better job. He says other workers join unions to fight for security, but he does not need to, because 'I don't think the job is a problem at all': so he worked when the union went on strike. The union's aims are not ours – we 'good skilled people' are in a minority, and the majority will not think about our welfare. 'A man who works properly can't get any benefit', because of union agreements. The government should improve living standards of 'ordinary people' – i.e. middle-income people like himself.

An older Christian has made a reasonable career for himself as a machine operator. After several years in the army, he was not getting promotion, so he left and went back to his land: he had property and was not worried. Then he and his wife both trained in a nearby Industrial Training Institute, and his wife qualified as a draftsman. (There are no 'draftswomen', she told me – just female draftsmen.) Meanwhile, they live with his family. Now they both work in the same factory. They will stay, because it would be difficult for both of them to find jobs elsewhere, and if only one of them was working, this would reduce their income. One of their daughters is in college, living at home, and they would like to find money to train her as a doctor. They have the standard middle-class complaint, the 'servant problem', since they need someone to look after the children and find local girls unreliable.

Everyone has a right to live, this couple think, and to that extent the communists who are illegally occupying forest land are justified. Inter-religious marriage is wrong. Marriage between Christians of different castes is all right if the two families are of similar origin, wealth and position: 'You have to keep up your own dignity' – if you gave your son or daughter in marriage to a poor labourer, you would not like to admit it.

A Brahman skilled worker in a public sector factory comes from a middle-class family, and was originally apprenticed to a garage. He complains that the union's agreement on promotion by seniority benefits the lazy but not hard workers like him: it is different in the private sector, where (he believes) the idle can be sacked. He employs a servant and has a good middle-class house, with a modern kitchen and plenty of furniture; he rents out part of it. Since he needs more money to educate his children, he organizes a tailoring chit fund (rotating credit association) for a commission, organizes sightseeing trips and pilgrimages by bus or car, and, with a partner, buys crashed cars and has them repaired for resale at a garage he knows. He hopes to develop this into a full-time business, or to become a building contractor.

Security versus opportunity

The right balance between security and opportunity is a practical problem confronting many workers who see possibilities of personal advancement but hesitate to take them. These risk-minimizers with a wistful eye on the job market are perhaps the largest group, after those who will stay where they are because they see no alternatives at all. Public sector workers see the contrast as one between public sector security and private sector opportunity; so do some in the private sector. There is some truth in this: private sector wages are higher, and there may be more promotion on 'merit'; it is easier, but not much easier, for private managements in the large modern factories to sack workers; and in the long run there is a risk that a private factory will close down. Of course the main counterattraction to security is income. Other workers think of leaving their jobs for more pleasant conditions, or less monotonous work, or for special personal reasons, but they hesitate to take the risk.

Subraman'iam, a middle-caste Tamil of about 30, is the son of a small-town teacher. After SSLC he took the Intermediate Science examination at a college near his town, hoping to be a doctor, but could not afford to continue (or failed?). He kept the family's grocery shop for seven years, while looking for a better job. His brother-in-law advised him to get a government job, because 'business can bring you to the pit, and pull your legs also' (as Subraman'iam said in English). Finally he got into a Bangalore public sector factory – on merit, he says, without any recommendation from his brother-in-law who works there. He took a diploma in mechanical engineering by attending evening classes at the factory; and after seven years' service, he was selected for an apprenticeship, his salary (the median for this factory) being 'protected'. In the long run he hopes to take an engineering qualification, with which he says he could get a job anywhere; but the public sector is best, because 'some safety is there'.

He is married, with two sons; and he has brought two younger brothers (one married, with children) to Bangalore, where they work in the same factory. Presumably he helped them to find jobs. Altogether eleven people

Security versus opportunity

live in his two-room apartment. He manages all his brothers' wages and sends some money to their parents. The brothers hope to stay as a joint family, and would like to buy a house site.

Caste should go – all are equal, Subraman iam says; but it is hard to marry out of caste, because one's elders would object. What should be done in India over the next ten years? 'Poverty should be eliminated completely', food prices reduced, education improved and unemployment ended. How? We must work hard, and the government must take steps. What steps? 'I will have to think and tell you.'

Kumaar is a Harijan chargehand (lowest-level supervisor) in a public sector factory, about 35 years old. Like many educated Harijans, he comes from an army family. Kumaar left an English-language army school at 17 without much idea of what to do, and got the one job he applied for. He has operated various machines in the last sixteen years, and has certificates for courses in quality control, tool design etc. He explained his work by referring to an American book, *Machine shop theory and practice*, which he keeps at home.

He finds the public sector frustrating: the worker is not expected to know anything about his machine or the part he makes. Promotion depends on seniority and obedience, not efficiency and production. Wages are too low because the public sector recruits too many workers to reduce unemployment, and so the results of a few workers' efficiency are shared among the ineffi-cient. He has had small rewards for suggesting productivity improvements, and was working on a project for a new tool when I met him. But he says this will get him no promotion in the public sector – he would like to join one of the big private firms, 'where a job could be secure, and responsibility should give power also', and where he would be properly paid. But 'getting a job is like meeting God', so he applied (unsuccessfully) for assistance in starting a small ancillary industry.

Kumaar has been active in the union, politics and social work (I heard about his activities from others) and has a politico-religious ideology of serving God through social service. He was union assistant secretary for several years, and he thinks the pressure of union work is the reason he had only three promotions when others with the same length of service had five or six. A union official can easily get promotion by using his influence with the foremen and officers, but this means he must sacrifice some of the employees' 'rights and needs' and must not press their claims. A unionist who takes the 'straight route' will not get good confidential reports.

Three years ago he decided not to contest the union election, because Kannad'a language feeling ran high and as a Tamil he would not be re-elected: since then he has been promoted to chargehand. He supports no party but organizes election campaigns in his neighbourhood for candidates he approves of (with some success). He regards the old Congress as corrupt. (Like many people he returns constantly to the big moral issue of corruption.) The new Congress is better, but has not done as much for the poor as one might expect: they should have seized all Rs 100 notes to bring out 'black

111

money', and bank nationalization has not yet benefited the 'poor' – the workers should have been given loans to start their own businesses. Ordinary workers should not have to pay income tax.

Kumaar is married and has a small son. He thinks caste is 'a nuisance' and should go, but he has not suffered because of his caste; people mix freely in his neighbourhood, and intercaste love marriages are beginning to happen. He no longer goes to temples, because it is like 'cheating God', who created the world and sees all that happens in it. The best service to God is 'social work', educating other people and so on. To this end he has started an association of some forty young men who maintain a free reading room, named after the late DMK leader Annadurai, with a supply of Tamil books and newspapers; he does not belong to the DMK, but likes quoting Annadurai's maxims about befriending one's enemies, public responsibility and working to uplift the poor. The important thing – in public life as in industry – is 'understanding', good human relations, which avoids all conflicts: when the workers under him do good work, he personally thanks them and gets them tea. 'A word of appreciation' is more important than a money reward (though evidently he thinks he deserves more money himself).

Daniel is a Protestant semi-skilled worker of about 25 in a private factory. He left school without SSLC and did three jobs, before his brother's wife asked an engineer to give him a job in this factory. His Hindu wife, like her relatives, works in the same factory. If he works hard, he says, his supervisor may give him an increment. He has applied to the municipality for a retail shop in a new building, where he can work in the evenings. If it succeeds he might leave the factory, he says. (But I do not think he will.)

Dhanaraaj, a Harijan of about 30, is a group leader. The son of a small farmer, he went to a high school in Bangalore on a government scholarship (presumably a Scheduled Caste scholarship) and left with SSLC. He did many jobs, mainly in small workshops, and learned welding; he got his present job through a newspaper advertisement. Four years later he was promoted to group leader, supervising ten workers, instructing them, repairing and maintaining machinery and so on. He finds the work interesting and varied, unlike routine production jobs. He and a friend started a small fabrication and sheet-metal business, with rented equipment, where they worked in the evenings, but this failed. He helped to found the union, but resigned from union office when some workers shouted abuse at him: then he decided to 'come up' through hard work only. If he can raise the capital he would like to start another workshop without partners and will wait and see whether it is worth giving up his full-time job. On Sundays he rehearses plays in different Indian languages with a drama group from his factory; this is where I first met him.

His family married him to his elder sister's daughter, who is still at school. They are trying to find their own house, as it is evidently a strain for them to live with his elder brother, a less educated, semi-skilled worker in another factory, who has bought a good house on favourable terms through his firm. No one in the family has married out of caste: Dhanaraaj says intercaste marriages often break up, because the couple will not be used to each other's customs, and, if the husband has an accident, they can no longer turn to their parents for help. In a way intermarriage is a good thing, and the government should encourage it, for example by providing scholarships for the children. (One state government gives grants to non-Harijans marrying Harijans.) If a man from a 'backward community' married a Brahman girl, he too might become clever. In town things are '99 per cent' all right for Harijans; other people will accept Harijans into their houses (as his neighbours do), but it is very hard for Harijans in the villages: they cannot insist on their rights because they depend on other castes for work, or even visit the village 'hotel' (the word for 'café' in Indian languages). He prefers the city. Harijans must have some power and be bold, he thinks; then no one will trouble them.

Gangaadharan, a Harijan of about 35, is a skilled man in a public sector factory. The son of a millhand, he left school with SSLC, and got a job through 'influence'. (Few men admit this.) Promotion was slow, because then that too depended on 'influence', though now it depends more on seniority. He is critical of workers who are lazy, and supervisors who just sit at a table. India needs a strong government which will impose discipline and make people work hard.

Gangaadharan is married, with a baby daughter, and can only just manage on his wages: so the big question is whether he can find a better job without loss of security – he is trying for one at another government factory, or a better job in his present factory: he would like to work with computers. (I made sure he knew the general principles of computers.) In the long run, he says, the only important thing is to be happy with one's family. Caste feeling is not too much of a problem for him, though as a Tamil he is apprehensive about language feeling among unemployed Kannad igas. Intercaste marriage is 'scientifically' good – mentally and physically – and is coming.

A man who feels this security–opportunity dilemma acutely is Krisn'amuurti, a 50-year-old Brahman in a supervisory job. His father had 'some business' in Bangalore. When Krisn'amuurti left school at 16 he wanted to learn automobile engineering, but his family told him people could do without cars but would always need clothes, so they apprenticed him to a tailor. He had his own tailoring firm with nine employees; but though he earned good money he could never keep it, whether he made fifty or a thousand rupees a month, and he had no prospect of pension. So twelve years ago he took a supervisory job in a factory. But here he is 'a slave': he used to work long hours but could fix them himself – even as an apprentice he could come and go when he liked, because he was unpaid. Since childhood he has been used to independence. He took his present job because of 'unavoidable circumstances' – I think because he needs Rs 15 000 to marry off his daughter. When he qualifies for retirement benefit, 'I will adjust here and there, and I will celebrate the marriage.' Then he can be a free man, and start his own business again, tailoring and selling cloth. (It is hard to say whether he seriously intends to do this, or whether it is a dream he was filling out for a sympathetic inquirer.) He says he himself can live independently, go anywhere, and earn his living as a tailor: but that his sons – or at least one of them – trained only for a job in this factory.

Krisn'amuurti rents a fairly large house near the factory, where he lives with his wife, his daughter who has studied typing and now stays at home waiting to be married, and his two sons, who work in the same factory. Asking the children about their lives and work was difficult, because their father often answered for them, telling me just what they wanted and planned to do, while the sons stood respectfully in their father's presence. Both sons will stay in the factory unless and until they can get something better, anywhere. (The younger was awaiting the result of a commerce degree examination.) Many of Krisn'amuurti's relatives are professionals. Though circumstances forced him to move away from his two brothers, he would like his sons to stay with him as a joint family if possible. They will all marry into the same Brahman subcaste, of course, though he claims he has friends of all communities.

Factory employment as a stage or incident before a career

For the minority of ambitious, motivated men who see factory employment as a stepping-stone to better things (realistically or not), there is a more or less loose practical relation between what they do in the factory and what they hope to do afterwards. Technical training and experience with machines will be useful when they start their own workshops; contacts with factory officers will help them to get contracts for the supply of components; union work is useful for those who want a union or political career. For these people the job is not the same as the career. The important thing is the career, that part of a lifetime in which an individual moves through a series of positions in the economy: the shape of a *lifetime* is roughly that of this career.

For some other factory workers, the shape of a lifetime is also that of a career, but their present job has a more or less accidental relation to the real, structured career which has not yet begun – except to the extent that factory work provides them with the means to live, look around and make plans. Factory employment puts them into a lower-middle class, or maintains them in it, allowing them the middle-class luxury of choice.

Kempayya is a semi-skilled worker in a public sector factory. The son of a middle-caste farmer, he left school with SSLC at the age of 22. His father

Factory employment before a career

wanted him to farm the family land, but Kempayya wanted to get away. He took a 'casual' job as a wireman in Bangalore, which lasted for seven years. Then he got his present job through a newspaper advertisement. He was active in the communist union and got into trouble with the management; so he decided a quiet life was best, joined the 'recognized' union, and was a union official for some time. Now he does not want to be much involved with the union, or with politics; he says he is just an ordinary member and cultivates his garden. This he does with great success: since he works shifts, he spends much of the daytime growing vegetables around his house in the factory township, and makes a modest income by selling them. He is a farmer at heart, and constantly says so. In busy agricultural seasons he takes leave to go to the twenty-two-acre farm he shares with two brothers, twenty miles away; he brings back grain for his family and about Rs 400 a year. His ambition is to save a deposit for an American tractor and then go back to full-time farming. A farmer's life is better because no one gives orders or times your work: 'Everything is in our hands'. (But the brothers employ three or four labourers, to whom they presumably give orders.) After his first wife died in childbirth he married an unrelated woman of his caste, from a big house in the urbanized village near the factory, and they have three young children. I was unable to find out what she thought of his plans, as she was staying with her family.

Prabhaakar is a skilled worker in a private factory, about 30 years old. I met him at a Sunday morning rehearsal of a 'social' drama in Kannada put on by the factory's drama group. Prabhaakar played a would-be actor showing off his talent, overacting, exhibiting anger and surprise and striking exaggerated attitudes. (I suspect the overacting was no caricature, but Prabhaakar's normal style.) I met him again in his two-room apartment in the city, where he lives with his wife, three young children, and his younger brother (who is employed as a 'learner' in a small workshop at a nominal Rs 18 a month).

His father farms five acres with labourers, and at one time had a small printing press in Madras City. Prabhaakar came to Bangalore at the age of 10 to live with his uncle, failed matriculation, and worked as a factory turner for two years. When his present factory opened, a foreman recommended him for a job, which he has held for ten years. But his real passion is acting: his walls are covered with photos of himself in different roles with amateur groups, and there are more in an album (e.g. of Prabhaakar in a kind of toga, in a play about Socrates). His roles include 'comedy, tragedy, old men, as well as lady characters'. He hopes for a job in films – either through a Kannada actor he knows in Bangalore, or through his brother-in-law, who is a lighting foreman in a Madras studio. He is not interested in going further in the factory. I think in fact that he is half serious about his intention, and is sufficiently screen-struck to leave his present job if he gets a firm offer of a job connected with films.

Prabhaakar is strongly for intercaste love marriage (a common film theme).

Some careers

He married for love, asking his wife's father. Since his wife belongs to a different subcaste of Naidus, he regards this as intercaste marriage. He would like his children to get a convent education and go into some technical line.

Middle-aged men, even men in their 30s, may have ambitions for a proper career to start when they retire at 58, or when they qualify for minimum retirement benefit after ten years' service, or longer if they need to accumulate capital.

Raajaraam, a skilled worker of about 35, is the son of a Brahman village accountant ten miles away. He commuted daily to a Bangalore secondary school, but left at 15 without SSLC and worked for six years in printing shops as a binder, machine operator and compositor in English and Kannad'a. Printing jobs were easy to get then. His last job was with a newspaper; the chief reporter recommended him to the manager of a public sector factory, where he was hired as a labourer and has worked his way up for fifteen years. He never had any formal training, but makes different components to precise blueprints. Whenever a new component is to be made, the time-and-motion men watch him or another worker, and use a stopwatch to estimate the time required for the job. The work is interesting but hard and sometimes dangerous; yet he has had no accidents. Recently he borrowed money from a co-operative bank to pay for a family ceremony, some furniture and to repair and paint his house. To save money he has stopped drinking, smokes bidis instead of cigarettes, and has coffee instead of a snack before work.

Altogether he has had enough: he is 'too old' to find another job, and can only think of retirement. He would resign tomorrow if he could, but at least he must pay his debt and save some capital. He plans to convert the front of his house into a bangle shop, and he expects his son (now aged 10) to help him with the shop: the son will then be 'independent', instead of going into a factory. His two daughters will marry: that is their career.

Raajaraam thinks (or says) he might arrange intercaste marriages for his children, because it is time to forget about caste in free India: everyone has the same blood. He was active in social work, politics and the campaign against cow slaughter, but has given up most of these activities because of family worries. As a Brahman he knows a little Sanskrit: he performs the regular brahmanical domestic ceremonies, and goes on pilgrimages.

The career as a stage or incident in a lifetime

For others the main thing in life is not their career at all. The career is bracketed away as a relatively unimportant series of incidents in a lifetime, which has meaning only as part of a larger scenario: often this is the career of the family, seen as a continuous development in which a man's life is only an incident.

One man, whose father was a tamarind merchant in a small way, had to leave the machine shop for a semi-clerical job with no prospects when he lost the sight of one eye in an accident. But what happens to him does not matter: his only interest is in seeing that his sons get a better education and jobs than his own. If they find jobs elsewhere, he takes it for granted that he will leave his job to live with them. For this man the career that counts is not his own but that of the family, especially the male line.

A few make religion the centre of everything. The job is just the means of subsistence, or a duty to be performed without attachment, so that they can concentrate on the religious life: meditation, worship and sectarian activities, or a neo-Hindu ideal of social service. One has freedom of choice in the things that matter, but the career is not one of these.

For many people, this ideal of non-attachment is a commonplace, the religious justification for a career in the world. For a very few, it is the whole point of living.

Nat'araajan, a Brahman toolmaker of about 35 whose relatives are middle-class professionals, took an engineering diploma and did three jobs before getting his present job in a private factory. He says he never used recommendations or influential relatives to get jobs. At one time he was against marriage and went to live with a Svaamijii (ascetic). Nat'araajan 'tortured' others by preaching brotherhood, until his brother told him he should marry. Now he is resigned to his marriage, and no longer regrets it. He also did voluntary work for the DMK party, since he was attracted to their ideal of a casteless society.

He got into serious trouble with a Madras firm when he fought for compensation for an old worker whom a supervisor injured with an iron bar; trouble with the caste for campaigning against dowry; trouble with his wife for his indifference to caste rules and rituals. He and three partners are trying to raise a bank loan to start their own toolroom, but his ideal (genuine, in his case) is the Giitaa's ideal of action without attachment to results: he should regret nothing, even if his own child died. He spends some time daily in meditation, and imagines his own previous life as a warrior in Kashmir – he does this 'for fun', just as he practises astrology and palmistry, but it is clear that he half believes it.

'Communalism': the community of birth and its common interest

Some factory workers – apparently not very many – see their interests as bound up with the common interest of some community of birth (caste or language group or religion), so that their own life chances depend mainly on the fortunes of the group. Other communities provide scapegoats. Of couse 'communalism' of one kind or another pervades many or most people's thinking: but there is a difference between the majority who believe, often rightly, that jobs and promotion depend partly on caste pressures and communal affinities, and the minority who see this, not as one factor weighing against others, but as the single explanation for every important step in one's career – and, especially, every failure.

Thus some Harijans see their best chance in protective discrimination and quotas, and hanker for Dr Ambedkar's neo-Buddhism without wanting the practical complications of conversion (mainly the loss of 'Scheduled Caste' privileges and concessions). Some Kannad̓igas support the Kannad̓a particularist parties (Chaluvaligars and Kannad̓a Paksha), and see their careers as blocked by clever Tamil and Malayali immigrants, or by Bangalore-born non-Kannad̓igas. There has been serious language trouble at one factory, where a few semi-skilled workers, with a larger number of unemployed at the gates demanding jobs for Kannad̓igas, beat up non-Kannad̓a workers, until dismissals and police action put a stop to the riots. Others blame setbacks on Sindhi refugees, Marwari money-lenders, Hindus (if they are Christians or Muslims), non-Brahmans (if they are Brahmans), Brahmans (if they are not) and so on.

A Lingaayat variant of the Protestant ethic?

My last example seems to be a variant of the Protestant ethic of work as a calling, among workers belonging to the Lingaayat or Viirashaiva sect. This Hindu sect began in the twelfth century as a protest against Brahman supremacy and the rigours of caste and ritualism, and partly adapted itself to the caste society without losing all its original features. The sect is strongest in Mysore, where Lingaayat castes dominate a large part of the state and play an important part in politics. I have a sample of only three Lingaayat workers, all from one factory; but I find them very interesting.

Lingaraaj is a senior draftsman of about 35, belonging to a Lingaayat Weaver caste. He is married, with two young children. His wife kept out of the way when I called. Inside the door of his small house in the township, he keeps the new scooter he is buying with a loan from the factory.

His grandfather was a handloom weaver, and his father a master weaver in another town. Lingaraaj left school with SSLC at 21, and went to Dharwar town to study commercial art under a painter. He earned a little by painting signboards; but since he was getting nowhere, he went home and found a temporary job as clerk to a weavers' co-operative while he looked for a proper job. The painter who had taught him eventually encouraged him to apply to his present factory, and I think may have helped to get him the job. He painted machinery, wrote signs etc., until the paint affected his health, and he qualified as a draftsman. He once tried to start a small work-shop with a partner, and might try again if he gets capital; but he will probably stay and expects to become a supervisor. He is active in the Social Welfare (or mutual benefit) Society supported by the management and was in charge of fund-raising for a temple and marriage hall for all Hindu com-munities in the township. He is a keen photographer.

Lingaraaj has read some Hindu philosophy, and can explain the difference between dualist and non-dualist theology; though he says philosophy is like elastic, and anyone who knows much about it can twist it in different direc-tions. Baasava, the founder or reformer of the Lingaayat sect, was 'like us', married (i.e. not a renouncer like other gurus), but 'perfect in his life'. He was born a Brahman, but 'got rid of all those dirty things' – caste pride and quarrelling, ideas of high and low etc. He was against untouchability because all are one and equal before God. Baasava taught that it is a sin to eat without working and to depend on others, so he worked as a clerk in the king's treasury. By intelligence and hard work he rose to be the king's prime minister, and purified society. Now distinctions of high and low caste have crept back among the Lingaayats, so they must reform again. In fact Lingaraaj is quite conservative in his practice: he thinks a man whose house he once ate in may be low caste (this is almost the extent of his liberalism); and he was upset by Jacqueline Kennedy's remarriage (though Lingaayats have not always been against widow remarriage, as the more brahmanized castes are). Those who need money should ask those who have it to give it voluntarily; the communists are wrong because they will rob you, and your sorrow will affect the robber as well.

Rudrappa, a machine operator, about 35, lives nearby in a house with care-fully tended flowers and creepers around the door. His brothers now farm the family's four acres and keep silkworms in a village. Rudrappa completed his education at a town near the village, and left school at 20 with SSLC. He wanted to study further and to become an accountant, but he could not afford to; so he took a relative's advice and applied to his present factory, which kept him waiting for fourteen months while he worked on the farm. He now sees that his relative was right: technical work pays better than an office job. He joined the factory as a helper, and later trained as a milling-machine operator. Clearly he is a conscientious, careful worker, who des-cribes his work, timings and productive innovations in minute detail. He also earns commission by running a chit fund and an insurance agency.

He says the Lingaayats' 'customs and duties' are different from those of other castes, being strictly non-violent, vegetarian and teetotal. His friends are of different communities but he cannot eat in their houses, because they eat mutton, which would make Lingaayats vomit. He is active in the Lin-gaayat Association – one of the caste and linguistic associations encouraged by the management, each having a factory officer of the right community as

Some careers

its president. Baasava, he says, was a 'political leader', being a minister. While serving in that post he became a philosopher, the main point of his philosophy being that all men are one and should not be divided.

Rudrappa lays great stress on hard work, mutual aid through voluntary associations, and living within one's income. He prefers the 'recognized' union to its more militant rival, because it is better to co-operate with the management. His wife was sterilized after giving birth to her third child, according to 'government regulations' (i.e. government encouragement), because one should have only as many children as one can afford to educate properly. As long as his children are well educated, they will find jobs: he has no job in mind for them.

These brief accounts of some long conversations cannot give the impression of a special kind of character: ethical, conscientious and even meticulous, moderately ambitious, equalitarian in principle but conservative in practice; lutheran rather than calvinist,[6] conscientious rather than enterprising, just as their theology of grace and practical devotion contrasts with the determinism of the brahmanical non-dualist tradition. These Lingaayat factory workers emphasize Baasava's dual role: as a career man, who rose in the king's service by hard loyal work and intelligence; and as a mystical poet and a religious and social reformer. On the one hand they have an ideology of careful work and deserved promotion within the organization, and they seem to identify with Baasava's career or to take it as a model. But they are not literal minded, they have a genuine feeling for Baasava's mystical theology, his religious and moral universalism and his devotional poetry in Kannad'a. I do not know enough about Lingaayatism to explore the connexion between the religious ideology and careers, or to say whether this double character of Baasava is traditional or an adaptation to the situation of Lingaayats working in a modern bureaucratic organization.[7] I have treated them at such length partly

[6] See M. Weber, *The Protestant ethic and the spirit of capitalism* (London, 1930).
[7] For a perceptive study of Lingaayat ideology, see C. Parvathamma, *Politics and religion: a study of historical interaction between socio-political relationships in a Mysore village* (New Delhi, 1971), especially on the Lingaayat attitude to work: 'The Lingayat rose above the Brahmanical notions [of purity] to regard "work" as essential to earn a living' (p. 86). 'Basava and his followers emphasized that every one should follow a vocation to earn his living. A vocation or work was considered very necessary to realise one's salvation. Work is heaven, *kayakave kailasa*, irrespective of notions of "low and high" status thus provided the real liberal ethics for work...For Basava descried the rigid occupational structure and caste hierarchy found in Brahmanical Hinduism. His emphasis was not on the nature of work but on one's devotion to any kind of work followed as a vocation in life' (pp. 114f.) A. K. Ramanujan discusses the idea that 'work is heaven' in

because, if there is an emergent type of character and ideology among the many middle-class, middle-caste factory workers, then these Lingaayat workers express it most clearly: an attitude that is both 'traditional' and 'modern' (if those words mean anything), idealistic, reforming, moderately equalitarian from within the security of the citadel, putting a high value on hard work, consistency, and sincerity and purity of intention.

the introduction to his translations of Lingaayat lyrics, *Speaking of Śiva* (Harmondsworth, 1973), p. 35.

This rejection of relativist caste morality, and the reinterpretation of high-caste notions of purity as inner purity attainable by all, is not new to Hinduism, though it is often regarded as something radically inconsistent with Hindu ethics. Weber was only half right when he wrote: 'The pious Hindu could advance in the scale of transmigration only by the strictly traditional fulfilment of the duties of the caste of his birth. . .The Indian ethic is in this respect the most completely consistent antithesis of the Puritan, as in another respect (traditionalism of the caste structure) it is opposed to the Hebrew' (*Protestant ethic*, p. 265). But the two tendencies – towards a closed relativist morality of groups, and an open universalist morality – have long coexisted in India, in unresolved contradiction. Early Lingaayatism is just one of the most notable attempts to tilt the balance towards moral universalism. It is relevant that the British called the Lingaayats 'the puritans of the East' (Parvathamma, *Politics and religion*, p. 86).

5
The structure of a career

These shortened accounts of careers show some common themes and contrasts: like the contrast between personal advancement and security, or the theme of the organized sector as a citadel of security and relative prosperity. On the whole these reflect realistic judgments of the situation as I see it.

This chapter is an experiment in analyzing the structure of careers from the workers' point of view, taking their categories and distinctions as a starting point, rather than a description of their situation seen from outside (which would begin with characteristics of the work force, actual recruitment policies, technology etc.). Both approaches are needed if we are to explain action by the logic of the situation, because people's understanding of their situation depends partly on the results of previous actions, and these results depend on whether their assessment of the situation was correct or not. 'If people define situations as real, they are real in their consequences';[1] but there is an external, independent reality all the same, and people have to adjust their definitions of what is real as they come up against this reality.

Clearly these typical structures in workers' thought do not represent a consensus on all important questions of fact and value, shared by a 'society' or a homogeneous group. They are the gist of many individual accounts, given separately and *ad hoc* to a stranger in an unfamiliar situation, and grouped according to rough similarities in structure and emphasis and the kinds of situation in which they make sense: what is rational for a skilled middle-class worker to expect is not so for an unskilled man with no chance of promotion; the Lingaayats' cultural heritage affects the way they see their situation; and so on.

Each account is affected by the special situation in which it was given to me. To the extent that it is authentic thought (and I believe most workers tried to tell the truth, on the whole), it represents a

[1] H. Beynon and R. M. Blackburn, *Perceptions of work: variations within a factory* (Cambridge, 1972), p. 3.

moment in a flux of thinking and acting, as often as a settled, considered opinion. A man's past is seen as relative to his problems now. And it is at moments of crisis and choice, rather than on the plateaux of stability, that ideas are revised and crystallize in new forms. When there are discrepancies and contradictions, some do not matter much because they are offhand, speculative opinions; others point to rationalizations, and serious practical or moral or intellectual problems confronting the speaker.

These are the steps in analyzing workers' accounts of their careers: first, distinguish the standing of different statements, ranging from lies, through offhand rationalizations, isolated reasoned explanations of actions, coherent and apparently sincere arguments which emerge in the context of a conversation and explain the facts well, to fully thought-out arguments, deeply held convictions and ideologies. The criteria for doing this include the statements' relation to observed actions and external facts, and their logical coherence. The decision must be partly a matter of personal judgment, taking into account the nature of the informant's temporary relation to me. (Am I a guest in his house? How often have I met him and in what company? and so on.)

Secondly, identify his significant distinctions and categories of people: castes, classes (and the special meaning of 'class' as an urban Indian category), good/bad, generous/mean, influential/dependent, deserving respect or contempt or pity etc.[2]

Lastly, trace the internal structure of the argument in each man's account of his career. To bring out these structures I have tried to

[2] 'There are several reasons why social anthropologists studying Indian society at the grass roots (as many like to believe) have bypassed problems of this nature [about class]. The most plausible methodological justification offered is that the problems of social anthropology are best studied in terms of native categories – by following the grain of the society, as it were – and that categories of the class type, not being native categories in the Indian context, cannot be handled in this fashion. . .Ignoring for the time being the fact that there are many conceptions of class (as there must be of any fundamental social category). . .there is a whole range of Bengali terms. . .and their counterparts in other Indian languages which are directly relevant to the analysis of what sociologists understand by class. These are not merely terms imported into the countryside by party theoreticians, but constitute categories used by the villagers to define a significant part of their social universe, to identify themselves and others and to act in a variety of contexts on the basis of these identities.' (A. Béteille, 'Peasant associations and the agrarian class structure', *Contributions to Indian Sociology*, new series, 4 (1970), 126–39 (p. 138); and see Béteille's 'Ideas and interests: some conceptual problems in the study of social stratification in rural India', *International Social Science Journal*, 21:2 (1969), 219–35.)

relate each statement to a three-dimensional scheme. (But this is no more than an experimental device, a list of things and relations to look for.) I find this a helpful way to contrast types of careers; for those who find it unhelpful, the main argument about each type is summed up in the notes under the diagrams.

One dimension is *time*. Moving outwards in both directions (past and future) a job is seen as part of a career, which is part of a lifetime, which is part of a family line extending over generations. (Or a series of rebirths, or some long-term historical entity like the Nation or Progress or the 'struggle of the working class': but for most people this is much less important.) This is like the syntagmatic axis of structural linguistics, because a man can only have one main job at a time, or one career at a time, or one life at a time.[3]

The second dimension (paradigmatic?) is *systems of relations*. At each point in his account, the informant sees himself in relation to certain other people, and these relations impose roles on him. Whether he identifies with these people or not, these are the ones he has most to do with, and his relations with them are practically and morally important to him. In his job he is involved with people doing other jobs in the factory. (To put it another way: his job is a special role; the system of relations is a role-set, 'the group of relationships associated with a particular role'.)[4] His career is the way he thinks of all the work he does in a lifetime, as a line leading somewhere. It is an alternative to other possible careers, and involves him in relations with people having similar or complementary careers: so his career is a place in the Indian economy and class structure. His 'lifetime' is more than his working career. When he thinks on this time scale, he sees himself as involved in systems of personal relations, especially with kin, also with

[3] 'Why do we say that the phrase *my new car* in English consists of three elements (three words) rather than, say, of four or two? The answer, according to Saussure, rests upon the notion of substitutability. We can substitute *the, his, that*, etc. for *my* in the first position; *old, beautiful*, etc. for *new* in the second position; and *picture, book*, etc. for *car* in the third position. There are three, and only three, places where the operation of substitution can be carried out (at this level of analysis). Sets of elements which can be substituted one for another in a given context are said to be in *paradigmatic* relationship; elements which combine to form a larger unit are said to be in *syntagmatic* relationship.' (J. Lyons (ed.), *New horizons in linguistics* (Harmondsworth, 1970), 'Introduction', p. 16.)

[4] D. Emmet, *Rules, roles and relations* (London, 1966), p. 140.

   'Job' is ambiguous. It usually means an 'employment relation', or all the work a man does for one firm; but he may sometimes think of promotion or transfer to another kind of work in the same firm as a new job. I am grateful to R. P. Dore for pointing out this ambiguity.

the caste, fellow workers, friends etc. The longer time scale, 'generations' (or Progress etc.), belongs to some conception of a universal
moral order, perhaps.

The third dimension is *judgments of fact and value*. A statement may
be the informant's view of what is; or of what might be – conceivable
alternatives, whether these are evaluated or not; or his ideal view –
what ought to be. An ideology relates judgments of fact and value, in a
more or less coherent view of the world as it is, and might be, and
should be.

The ideal view must sometimes be inferred from statements about
time. Traditionally 'was' often means 'should be', because it is axio-
matic that we live in an age of degeneration, the Kaliyuga: the time
axis has to be rotated on to the is/ought axis.[5] Now 'will be' sometimes
means 'should be', because people believe in Progress. But since most
urban Indians now believe, part-time, both in degeneration and Progress, we may have a U-shaped curve: either 'was' or 'will be' means
'should be', according to context.

One reason why the possible view must be distinguished here is that
the conceivable forms of industrial organization cannot be taken as
given (e.g. as capitalism) or limited to a few *existing* alternatives (like
America, Russia, Japan, China). The present Indian system is welfare
capitalism, kept in check by government regulation, strong unions and
to some extent by the welfare ideology of the managing class, and
mixed with state enterprise (not very different in practice). A more
ruthless, old-fashioned capitalism exists, but does not directly affect
the people studied here, who work in the organized sector covered by
Factory Acts, Employees' State Insurance etc.

The first of my three questions (factory workers' place in Indian
society: are they an élite? etc.) is to be answered mainly from the
observer's point of view; it is an objective question. The third (about
the idea of a 'job' and a 'career'), from the informant's point of view
(as he sees the situation, and thinks it should and might be). The
second (factory workers' understanding of their situation) needs an
answer from both points of view together, matching the workers' own
thought to social reality as it appears to an outsider.

[5] This is why foreigners are easily misled into taking literally the people's statements
about the 'traditional' Indian family, village organization etc. – how people say it
was in the past. One is not dealing with memories at all, even distorted memories,
but with ideals expressed in conventional form, as 'history'. On Indian conceptions
of time and change, see D. F. Pocock, 'The anthropology of time-reckoning',
Contributions to Indian Sociology, 7 (1964), 18–29; and J. V. Bondurant and M. W.
Fisher, 'The concept of change in Hindu, socialist and neo-gandhian thought' in
D. E. Smith (ed.), *South Asian politics and religion* (Princeton, 1966), pp. 235–48.

The structure of a career
Types of careers and arguments

Consider the structure of a career as some types of workers see it.
The Brahman clerk Naagaraajan put the characteristic argument of
the *paternalists* (or rather those who want paternalism; see pp. 88–95).
This can be figured in two of my three dimensions (time, and systems
of relations):[6]

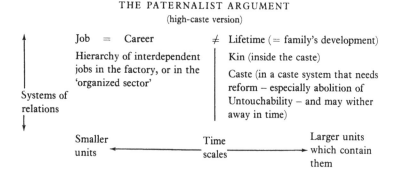

THE PATERNALIST ARGUMENT
(high-caste version)

Job = Career ≠ Lifetime (= family's development)

Hierarchy of interdependent / Kin (inside the caste)
jobs in the factory, or in the
'organized sector' / Caste (in a caste system that needs
reform – especially abolition of
Untouchability – and may wither
away in time)

Systems of relations

Smaller units ← Time scales → Larger units which contain them

The hierarchy of factory jobs is morally justified in the interests of the social
whole (as in the traditional holistic ideology of caste). 'Is' = 'ought' normally:
i.e. in an idealized past; in the organized sector now; and in a future when the
benefits of this type of organization will spread to those now excluded. To say
something will be is almost the same as saying it should be.

One has a limited degree of choice in making one's career. The development of the family, and family matters like marriage, are affected only
marginally, or not at all, by one's choices.

Aar·umugam, Naagaraajan's Harijan ('Untouchable') friend and
union colleague, sees it like this (see pp. 92–3):

[6] The horizontal line connects the different *time scales* which parts of a statement
may refer to. The movement from left to right is not the passage of time from
earlier to later or past to future (as it would be if the line corresponded more closely
to the syntagmatic axis), but a progression from smaller units to larger ones which
contain them (job, career, lifetime . . .). The equals sign (=) means the smaller
unit is integrated into the larger one in some logical or rational way; the 'is not
equal to' sign (≠) means the relation is seen as contingent or forced or accidental.
   The vertical line stands for systems of *social relations* a man is involved in, or
people he deals with. Each time scale imposes a role on him. If one unit is integ-
grated in a larger one (e.g. if job = career) then his roles, and the systems of
relations he plays these roles in, are the same or similar.
   The fact/value dimension is sometimes implied in the structure: thus a man's
account of his job is mainly his perception of what is, his account of his career, what
is and what might be or might have been; in talking about his lifetime, he is
generally more concerned with what should be. Where it is not obvious, the distinction between judgments of fact and value must be spelled out.

Types of careers and arguments

THE PATERNALIST ARGUMENT
(low-caste version)

Job	=	Career	=	Lifetime	=	Family's development
Hierarchy in the factory				Other industrial workers (e.g. neighbours)		Movement towards a casteless and mobile society

The hierarchy of factory jobs is justified, but caste is not justified and never was. 'Is' never meant 'ought', but because of industrialization and nationalistic social reform the two are coming closer. Paternalistic factory organization (under a self-made managing director) is a framework in which one can make one's job and career by one's own efforts, and thus make one's family future and a more just and equal society. Marriage, friendship etc. are coming to be matters of choice not caste, and this is good.

Contrast the argument of the *militant unionists* (see pp. 95–8):

MILITANT UNIONISTS

Job	= or ≠	Career	≠	Lifetime	=	Historical movement towards revolution and socialism
Fellow workers, management		Fellow workers; one or several managements		The 'working class', esp. people sharing the same revolutionary ideals, inside or outside the organized sector		future society of equals

One's job and career depend more on impersonal market forces, employers, the state etc. than on one's own efforts, though effort and choice play a part. In the factory one interacts with fellow workers and the management; outside it, largely with other organized sector workers of similar opinions. Militants know that the 'working class' has a special position, and in some ways is a middle class; but members of the working/middle class, like their less fortunate comrades without steady jobs, are victims of a system that exploits them all. One's career is apart from one's lifetime, which has value and meaning to the extent that one works for equality and socialism. Socialism *will* and *should* come about: the long-term movement is from worse (exploitation) to better (socialism). 'Ought' will become 'is'.

This is an oversimplification. Few militants are so dedicated to the revolution, to the exclusion of the family, private interests etc. But this is their public argument; it cannot be dismissed, since it is the result of serious thought and discussion, and some of them *are* dedicated and *do* sacrifice personal and family interests to an ideal.

The structure of a career

Some other arguments are compromises between the two extremes of the paternalist argument and that of the militant unionists – like the argument of those who see their *career in the union or in politics* (see pp. 98–100):

A CAREER IN THE UNION OR IN POLITICS

Job	≠	Career	=	Lifetime	(= ? reform? revolution? advancement of one's own family?)
Fellow workers		Union or political activists			(Moving into a different class? A classless – or less class-ridden – society?)

A man makes his own career. His present job is just a stage in building this career, to be left behind when he is firmly established in union office or politics. The important time scale is his *lifetime*.

It would be wrong to call these men 'careerists', which would imply they are self-interested or even cynical: many, perhaps most, of those I met are genuinely committed to an ideal of increasing social equality, a gradual broadening out of the benefits of industrial employment to the masses and so on; this is not inconsistent with wanting to advance their own careers and their families' position in the existing class structure (while it lasts).

The attitude of the cynics and self-seekers (the real careerists) is obvious. But it is too cynical, and a mistake, to ascribe cynicism to everyone else: most people's motives are mixed, anyway.

Idealistic, reforming, middle-class workers (see pp. 100–2) are also active in unions, and often in politics. This group are rather like the paternalists, except that they place less emphasis on hierarchy, more on equality, and (if they work in the public sector) on the moral superiority of working for the nation rather than private business, which pays better:

IDEALISTIC, REFORMING, MIDDLE-CLASS WORKERS

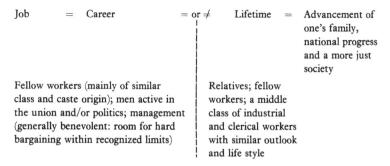

Job	=	Career	= or ≠	Lifetime	=	Advancement of one's family, national progress and a more just society
Fellow workers (mainly of similar class and caste origin); men active in the union and/or politics; management (generally benevolent: room for hard bargaining within recognized limits)				Relatives; fellow workers; a middle class of industrial and clerical workers with similar outlook and life style		

Types of careers and arguments

A man's career depends partly on his efforts, largely on economic forces beyond his control, and on management bureaucracies over which workers have some control – at least they can be negotiated with.

These people, who are sure of a job and usually some promotion, can allow themselves the luxury of a social conscience. They see few radical or irreconcilable contradictions in society: the sharp distinctions between classes and castes will be reduced by gradual economic development and social work by middle-class idealists like themselves, acting through a variety of associations, co-operatives, trade unions and sometimes the local branches of political parties.

Many but not all workers in the groups considered so far are 'middle class', relatively well educated, secure in their jobs and prospects, and with relatives in similar positions (though in most cases their standard of living would put them among the very poor in any European country). This is not simply a result of a middle-class bias in the sample interviewed, but because these 'middle-class' workers – including Harijans – form a large proportion of the organized sector work force, especially in the newer factories.

A group who are much less 'middle class' are the unskilled or semi-skilled, often low-caste workers, who see *no alternatives* to their present grade and little chance of promotion, and therefore give all their energies to staying where they are (see pp. 102–4):

NO ALTERNATIVES

Job	=	Career	= or ≠ Lifetime	(?)
Fellow workers, esp. in the same low grades			Kin, caste; friends, often from the same factory	(Not much concerned about the long term)

A man's career depends almost entirely on forces outside his control, and the decisions of another class. The main thing is to get one break in life, i.e. an organized sector job which is also a career: if promotion comes later, well and good.

This assessment is realistic. These people look after the short run and let the long run look after itself, which is rational in their situation. They never initiate collective action to improve the condition of factory workers, still less of 'society' on a grand scale. They need the union's help more for specific grievances, e.g. when the minimal promotion they can expect because of seniority is held up.

At the extreme are the few *hopeless cases*, who have difficulty in keeping the jobs they have (see pp. 104–5). They cannot even plan for the short term. What happens to them (as they see it) does not

The structure of a career

depend at all on their choices. Their social origins vary. Their problems are often special personal ones; in some cases, medical or psychiatric problems perhaps.

But others find their factory such a good place – friendly, secure, pleasant to work in – that they do not need to think about alternatives at all. They have no paternalist ideology; they are not ambitious; if they have long term social ideals, they see their factory (where 'is' and 'ought' are already one) as a model for a future society without harsh social distinctions. As long as they have security, they can concentrate on family and friends and colleagues and the pleasures of everyday life. They are lower-middle class and happy to remain so. These are the men who find the *factory a good place to work; why leave?* (see pp. 105–6).

The *factory owner's kith and kin* are a distinct group in one factory (see pp. 106–8). They share a common situation if not an ideology. This is how they tend to see their situation:

FACTORY OWNER'S KITH AND KIN

Job = Career	≠	Lifetime = Family's development
Others in their own group; fellow workers generally, and the factory hierarchy: neighbours in industrial suburbs – often immigrants to Bangalore like themselves		Kin, caste and others living in and about their (and the factory owner's) home town

There are few alternatives open to a young man in the small town these people come from. One's real career beings with one piece of good luck: a job in this factory, or another firm owned by the same man. Once in Bangalore, it is difficult to leave the factory, because of the owner's influence over one's family; but some people make a good career for themselves by working hard in this factory (which is one of the best payers in Bangalore).

These workers are more conservative, about matters like caste, than those from Bangalore itself or more politically conscious areas. They generally marry girls from their original place, found for them by their families, and keep close ties with their families. They are still young. I doubt whether they will go home for good, and their children will probably stay in Bangalore.

Those who put forward an *ideology of personal achievement* ('achievement-oriented' types – the vocabulary is not mine) are mostly young men from middle-class families, often with some technical training before they join the factory (see pp. 108–10):

130

AN IDEOLOGY OF PERSONAL ACHIEVEMENT

Job	$\neq$	Career	= Lifetime	(= Family's development?)
Factory hierarchy; fellow workers (mainly young and skilled); useful contacts (in factory, offices, anywhere) with a view to self-employment or a better job		Partners; aspiring executives	Upper-middle class (cosmo-politan, socially and geographi-cally mobile)	Esp. nuclear family

This is the structure of a career as it looks to them now. Since most of them are young, it represents aspirations for the future rather than distilled experience.

The important segment is 'career = lifetime'. The present job is just a preparation for this, and the sooner it is over the better. The longer term (the development of a family over generations) is not much present in their thoughts.

A career is something one makes for oneself, by one's own efforts. This *is* and *should be* so. Achievement has a moral value, and the reward is worldly success.

Hierarchies at work, and other social inequalities except caste, and justified by effort and achievement (though there is a hint that those from well-off influential families have a headstart). In their present jobs, these men have dealings with other factory workers by necessity, but prefer to move with people of similar ambition and background. They explicitly reject any soli-darity with the mass of factory workers, or the 'working class'. As soon as possible they hope to move into another circle altogether: the executive middle class. Some think of emigrating if they get the chance.

I think some of them will achieve what they aspire to, or part of it.

Their social ideal is a competitive free-enterprise economy, with a benevolent uncorrupt government and a strong nation. They are not very political.

I suggested that the second largest group (after those who see no alternatives at all) is probably made up of men who see chances of personal advancement but hesitate to take them, and for whom the question of *security versus opportunity* is a constant dilemma (see pp. 110–14). This is sometimes seen as possible choice between public sector security and private sector opportunity (including self-employ-ment):

The structure of a career

SECURITY VERSUS OPPORTUNITY

Job	$\neq$	Career	= Lifetime	= Family's development?
Fellow workers; management; contacts who might be useful if one tries some other line of work		Probably the same people – except that one *might*, just possibly, move into a different class and leave one's present associates behind		

The ideal is to make one's career by one's own efforts. The practical question which worries these men is whether they have a real chance of achieving what they see others have achieved. They are generally realistic about their chances: security comes first, and the dream of launching out into a better job or successful self-employment remains a dream. The lifetime is the time scale that matters.

This is an individualistic ideal. These men's social ideals are the usual well-meaning platitudes, not an ideology of aggressive individualism.

Those who see *factory employment as a stage or incident before a career* think of their 'career' as something which has yet to begin, and which will offer a more agreeable way of life, or more money and social advancement (see pp. 114–16). Factory work gives them an income and time to look round until this real, structured career can begin. Thus one would go back to farming; another would be a film star; and some talk as if their real career will begin when they have enough years of service to qualify for retirement benefit and invest it, for example, in a shop. This is how they see their situation:

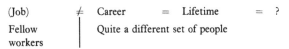

FACTORY EMPLOYMENT AS A STAGE OR INCIDENT
BEFORE A CAREER

(Job)	$\neq$	Career	= Lifetime	= ?
Fellow workers		Quite a different set of people		

The important thing is the career = lifetime; the 'job' is bracketed away, having little value in itself. Unlike the previous group, these people expect to achieve the kind of career they want, and make serious plans for it.

Or the whole working career may be bracketed away, as relatively unimportant in comparison with some long-term aim or higher truth, by the few men who see *the career as a stage or incident in a lifetime* (see pp. 116–17):

Types of careers and arguments

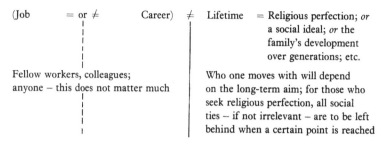

| (Job | = or ≠ | Career) | ≠ | Lifetime | = Religious perfection; *or* a social ideal; *or* the family's development over generations; etc. |

(Job = or ≠ Career) ≠ Lifetime = Religious perfection; *or* a social ideal; *or* the family's development over generations; etc.

Fellow workers, colleagues; anyone – this does not matter much

Who one moves with will depend on the long-term aim; for those who seek religious perfection, all social ties – if not irrelevant – are to be left behind when a certain point is reached

The '*communalists*' are those who believe that their interests are bound up with those of some community of birth (caste or religion or language), and that their careers depend on the fortunes of this group and are blocked by some other scapegoat community or communities (pp. 117–18):

'COMMUNALISM': THE COMMUNITY OF BIRTH AND
ITS COMMON INTEREST

Job	=	Career	=	Lifetime	=	Long-term interests of the 'community'
Fellow workers, esp. those of one's own 'community' (caste, language, religion), opposed to other 'communities'		The career depends on connexions and influence: one's castemen (or co-religionists etc.) in a position to give one promotion, a better job etc.		Network of relations inside the 'community'		The 'community' confronted with rivals and allies in a constant political and social struggle

One can struggle to achieve a decent life, but it is not much use tyring without the support of a powerful block. The block most conveniently to hand is the caste (which may correspond to a whole set of traditional caste-like groups, too fragmented for effective separate action in the modern situation), or the religion, language group etc. – any group one is born into, which is easy to distinguish from competing groups.

The point is that the 'caste system', justified by a religious ideology of purity and interdependence, has gone. The mask is off, there are only castes or other communities of birth, which give one the only protection and chance in a ruthlessly competitive market for power and scarce advantages – jobs, promotion, contracts. Unity is strength: moral obligations to outsiders would be an expensive luxury.

The structure of a career

This is very different from what seems to be *a Lingaayat variant of the Protestant ethic.* Although the Lingaayats are a caste (or a sect or a group of castes), these conscientious 'puritans' have a real commitment to moral and religious universalism (see pp. 118–21):

A LINGAAYAT VARIANT OF THE
PROTESTANT ETHIC?

Job	=	Career	=	Lifetime	=	Development of the family; moral perfection to be achieved through work; and a gradual movement towards a moral and prosperous society
Fellow workers; justified functional hierarchy in the factory; men involved in social work and religious associations (not only Lingaayats)		Often the same people: once established in a factory, it is generally best to work one's way up gradually through the hierarchy		Network of kin relations, mainly with Lingaayats, who are most numerous in another part of Mysore State		Other classes and groups; social work and religious devotion (each group to its own gods) will break down the barriers between groups

This ideology requires effort in one's calling and guarantees success. Like the Protestant ethic, it is effective: those who act on it are likely to do well in a functional hierarchy where skill and hard work count.

The different time scales are all of a piece. Job = career, because factory organization, promotion and training procedures etc. provide just the amount of opportunity these men are looking for. Success in a career, prosperity for one's family, a more moral society, religious perfection and mystical experience should and can go together. Social conflicts can be resolved by good will, the spread of true morality and religion, and industrialization. Radical conflicts of interest are a dangerous illusion. There is nothing *wrong* with caste, only with caste pride and competitiveness.

This is not a deterministic ideology: right action, feeling and doctrine can all be achieved by effort. If it is a Protestant ethic, it is lutheran rather than calvinist.

These are the main types of 'argument' about a career. They relate value judgments, or ends, to judgments of fact, and justify action. To see how far they *explain* action means taking into account other kinds of observation – of what people really do and the situation they are in – and relating these to what people say they do, and what they think their situation is.

Types of careers and arguments

This experiment in analysing and contrasting the ways in which different types of workers see their situation is an attempt to solve the problem mentioned at the beginning of chapter 4: How to communicate unique personal experiences, classify them and generalize about them, without fragmenting the individual accounts or distorting their meaning. In the next chapter I try, more ambitiously, to generalize about the direction of change in these people's thinking, and to place this change in its historical context.

6

Conclusions

This book is an attempt to develop an anthropology of urban work in India. I have tried to get away from the functionalist idea of bounded groups – factories or neighbourhoods – as systems of relations working towards some kind of balance, and from the oversimplifications of 'transactional' theory, towards a more dialectical account of industrial workers' situation, how they see their situation and what they make of it – not merely how they adjust to it, or how it determines their thinking.[1]

Chapter 1 raised some general questions about industrialization (pp. 1–3) and three particular questions about the minority of Indian workers employed in the new 'organized sector' factories. (pp. 3–4). In a pilot study there must be a gap between evidence and conclusions: the sample of workers is small but intensively studied, and I have used interviews with managers, statistical and census material and some knowledge of the Indian economic situation. These are my tentative answers to the three questions about the organized sector:

The first was: *Who are the factory workers, and are they a privileged élite?* This is largely a factual question, about workers' origins and their economic relation to other groups, especially 'unorganized sector' workers and country people.[2]

---

[1] cf. Beynon and Blackburn, *Perceptions of work*, p. 3: 'This attempt to release the study of worker involvement from the restrictions of a determinate organisational structure unites a group of theorists into what can be broadly termed the "action approach". Such an approach starts from the principle that if people define situations as real, they are real in their consequences. Thus, in what is perhaps the best known British application of this approach [J. H. Goldthorpe *et al.*, *The affluent worker: industrial attitudes and behaviour* (Cambridge, 1968), p. 184], the authors advocate using "a frame of reference within which the actors' own definitions of the situations in which they are engaged are taken as an inital basis for the explanation of their social behaviour and relationships . . . [which] would direct attention systematically to the *variety of meanings* which work may come to have for industrial employees."'

[2] The details are in chs. 2 and 3. On the question of whom the sample represents, see ch. 2, p. 26 ('the case study sample are not too untypical of the work force in

Conclusions

These factory workers come from a wide range of backgrounds, (urban and rural) and castes (including the small Harijan middle class, whose fathers or grandfathers were usually in the army or police), but very few from the poorest groups. Their incomes range with those of clerks and teachers: some of the people called 'middle class' in India. The things that distinguish them from men employed in small workshops and service establishments are (generally) income and (always) security: not a sharp break in life styles or attitudes.

The secondary benefits of factory employment are shared quite widely among workers' relatives, especially their parents, who get remittances, and the unemployed who come to live with them and find jobs through them; and there is a big multiplier effect because of factory workers' spending. In both cases the benefits go to a large part of the urban population, a substantial population in rural areas and small towns, but not much to the submerged mass of casual labourers and slum-dwellers.[3]

The second question was about *how factory workers see their situation.* They tend to see factory work as a citadel of security and relative prosperity, which it is: it offers regular work and promotion and predictable rewards, as against the chaos and terrifying dangers of life outside. For everyone inside the citadel, there is a regiment outside trying to scale the walls. Even educated Brahmans will take unskilled casual factory work in the hope of permanent jobs. Once inside the citadel, a man can look round for alternatives, if he wants.

This view of factory work as a citadel comes out especially in what workers say about the difficulty of getting a first factory job; about relatives and others without such jobs; and about the dangers of starting one's own business – something many of them would like to do if they dared.

This 'working class' is a 'middle class'. Workers are right to use these words interchangeably, as some do: even if a minority, stuck in the worst menial jobs, could hardly be called 'middle class'. It is a long time since office work conferred more status than well-paid manual work; anyway, an association with technology carries its own prestige. Many factory workers – like other employees in India's public and

the four factories studied. There is some bias towards the more educated, skilled and articulate workers ... but this bias has been quantified and can be allowed for. The four factories' work force is a fair sample of that in post-war "organized sector" factories in Bangalore and similar towns, where industrial expansion is recent and based on advanced technology.').

[3] My information about workers' origins is quite detailed; but these conclusions about relations with other groups are partial and based largely on impressions.

137

Conclusions

private bureaucracies – have a 'middle-class' life style and aspirations, some limited control over their own careers, and some power to defend their position by joint action (though not to improve it greatly).[4]

But factory workers, except those with an ideology of ruthless personal advancement or the 'divine right of the middle class', do not think of themselves as an élite or an aristocracy of labour by right. They are lucky and they know it. Recruitment and promotion are seen to be largely matters of luck, though some effort counts, too, and ought to count. Those who think in terms of a class struggle genuinely want to include the unemployed and casual labourers in their own group, on the unspoken assumption that their own position will not be affected. For those who do not think of a class struggle, their own position in relation to the poor is either a given unalterable fact, or something to be changed by benevolence and social work (which a few are actively involved in) or by all-round national economic progress.

Since these workers – especially the young educated ones – have middle-class aspirations and some real chance of upward mobility, there is not always a wide social gap between them and the management. Nor are their social origins always very different: some workers have close relatives in executive, official or professional positions, who may have helped them to get their present jobs. The managers and the managed do not live in two different worlds: the difference is between those who have succeeded and those who have not, or (if they are young and skilled) not yet.

One should not exaggerate: few workers become supervisors, and very few become managers, but some do. Indian industry, like British industry, has not seen a 'social democratic revolution' of the kind that happened to Japanese industry after the war.[5] Visible status distinctions in the factory are still sharp, not gradual; but they are not as rigid, and do not reflect such basic differences in ideas, as foreigners and Indians often think.

The third question was about the *idea of a 'job' and a 'career'*, i.e. how workers see their situation as individuals. A job is part of the career (or is the career), which is part of a lifetime, which is part of a family's development or some other long-term process. But different types of

[4] The 'middle class', in Indian usage, includes a few self-employed professionals and businessmen, and a much larger number of employees in bureaucratic organizations (including big firms), from highly trained professionals to clerks and technicians. Factory workers are, increasingly, in a similar situation. Everyone has security, and usually some chance of promotion. On the bureaucratic origins of this class, see B. B. Misra, *The Indian middle classes* (London, 1961).

[5] Dore, *British factory – Japanese factory*, pp. 115ff.

138

workers, with different experience or origins or personal opinions, relate these things in various ways (see chapter 5). The smaller unit may fit into the larger one in some rational, intelligible way: thus moving from job to job, or learning a skill and getting promotion, may add up to a career in which a man sees a pattern and meaning (either looking back, or planning or hoping for the future); his life may make sense because of his career; and so on. If there is a rational pattern in the progression from jobs to career to lifetime, it could be the result of choice and planning, or of cosmic or historical forces (like dharma or Progress): in either case the things that happen to a man have some meaning and value. Or the relation may be contingent, forced or accidental: he is pushed about by unpredictable forces, his career is just the sum of the jobs he can get, he makes a life for himself as best he can.

I can make some generalizations about the way these workers think of jobs and careers. Getting a first job in the organized sector is seen to depend mainly on luck. Choice and effort (e.g. at school, or in learning a trade in small workshops) can improve one's chances a little. Getting on inside the organized sector – whether in the same firm, or by changing jobs – depends on varying combinations of luck, influence, 'merit' assessed by others, and one's own planning and choice: the hardest choice is often between opportunity and security, but security usually wins. A career in the organized sector (unlike many outside it) is a line leading somewhere, not a random series of things that happen to a man.

The Japanese lifetime commitment to the firm is seldom or never found, even among the few 'paternalists': the necessary basic expectations are not there, on the part of workers or managements. A job is a job, and whoever gets a better one will take it.

Nor is a job property. The argument that Indian factory workers keep up a minimum standard of performance because they think of a job as something like the right to perform a customary service in the village jajmaani system may have been true in the past or in other places – not in Bangalore now.[6] The evidence used to support

[6] Thus Lambert writes, in his study of Poona factory workers in 1957, 'The carry-over of this general notion of reciprocal obligation between *jajman* and *purjan* into the factory, employer – employee is relatively easy.' (*Workers, factories and social change*, p. 92.) 'Most of the workers were interested in acquiring "permanent" property rights in a job and ... this carries with it a notion of minimal quality of performance but not an internalized drive for continuously enhanced productivity' (p. 179) – unlike factory workers elsewhere? 'Moreover, the general

that view can be explained as the result of management practices and/or the logic of the worker's situation inside the citadel, but with obligations to a number of people outside it.[7] The factory worker is not quite economic man minimizing risk, but much of his behaviour can be explained as the pursuit of a limited number of economic and other goals, and informants can often say specifically what they are: security, higher pay, easier or more interesting work, freedom from close supervision, a pleasant atmosphere at work, respectability, a better chance for one's children, socialism, work well done as a religious duty and so on.

This applies to the decisions a man makes about his work and career. But his career is not his whole life. Work occupies a much bigger place in some people's lives than in others. Everyone has his own world-view and hierarchy of values, though of course he usually shares these with others. In chapter 5 I discussed some of the ways in which different types of workers fit the objectives they try to realize through work into some integrated world-view: a model of society as it is and as it might and should be, justified by some implicit theory of human nature or some religious or political ideology.

Alternative models of man in society

I suggest – with caution – that in thinking about careers, marriage, personal relations, politics and religion, these people tend to place the individual at the centre of attention: as the free agent, the bearer of value, the point where social thinking begins. This implies a social contract theory: society, the state, economic institutions and the family exist and are justified because they reconcile the intentions of many individuals. This view of man is more relevant for more people in more situations than the alternative view of man as having value because of his place in a pre-existing social organism.

One can understand this change in emphasis, in a situation where people envisage the possibility of choosing their own lives and social relationships to a much greater extent than before: even if the real chances of choosing one's life are not *much* wider for most people, and most careers are determined by economic necessity and luck.

But to understand what is happening is not to show that it must happen. It might have been otherwise, 'industrial society' is probably compatible with many ideologies, and these ideologies may be worked

impression one gets in reading the literature on Indian factory labourers and in talking with factory managers is that a factory job is a form of property to the worker and that he will seek to retain, but not improve it' (*ibid.*).

[7] As in Morris, *Emergence of an industrial labor force*.

out in many different institutional forms. Thus either nuclear or extended family households can exist in peasant, pre-industrial urban or industrial societies: it depends on the particular conjunction of history, ideas and material circumstances.[8] But it is clearly *more likely* that people will want independence for the smaller unit – if they did not have it already – when important roles are separated out, not combined in many-stranded relationships; and when these roles are achieved, not ascribed, in principle and sometimes in practice.

This emphasis on choice has something to do with political and social movements; foreign models; new career patterns, social and geographical mobility; and the changing balance of numbers, education and earning power between generations. But the idea of choice is not new: only the things it applies to. Thus if people want or expect to choose their own marriage partners, or expect their children to do so, they are assimilating marriage to the traditional ideal of friendship, not of relations within a hierarchical structure.

It is a mistake to see this shift in emphasis either as a necessary part of the package which comes with industrialization, or simply as an import of foreign ideas. It would be more useful to see it as the latest stage in a dialectic which has been worked out in Indian society for a very long time: a conflict between two models of man's place in society and the universe. These two models – constantly acting on and modifying each other – have played different parts in the ideologies of classes, castes and sects at different periods in Indian history: but there is a continuous thread running through them. These are the terms in which the great debates about social relations, politics and religion have been conducted, whether on the level of ideas implicit in action, of popular thought and home-made sociology, or the great religious doctrines and controversies.

In one model, man's life has meaning and value to the extent that he identifies his will with his role in a social organism, which is part of a universal organism. Each part is necessary to the whole; and all the parts stand in a hierarchical relation, in which the higher 'encompasses' (Dumont's term) those below it. 'Parts' means individuals, or castes, or stages of life, or events, or any other particular things. Ideally, every human relation should be seen in its hierarchical context. Choice is reduced to a minimum: one has only to perceive one's true nature, and the true nature of the situation, to know what *must* be done.

[8] On this question, with special reference to pre-industrial England, see P. Laslett, *The world we have lost* (London, 1965).

Conclusions

This holistic, hierarchical model has been the dominant ideology throughout most of Indian history – but not the only one; it has always been open to critical attack from classes, religious sects or social movements, using the weapons provided by an alternative, subversive tradition. In the alternative model, individual people and events have meaning and value, choice is real, relations of equality are normal, and no permanent given structure has absolute value. In religion, this tradition is bhakti, the devotional and sectarian movement which usually begins with the sannyaasi, and which devalues caste in a religious context.[9] But in India religious and social movements are inseparable: movements critical of caste dominance (like the Sikhs and Lingaayats) were also bhakti sects, which were only partly reabsorbed into caste society.

So I propose this way of interpreting changes in values and social relations in modern India, especially but not only in Indian industrial society: A tradition of choice and equality, which is very old but was marginal, is becoming central, because it is more relevant to the situation and aspirations of new classes or kinds of people. A hierarchical, organic tradition, which was dominant, is becoming marginal instead. But neither tradition is static. These two traditions correspond to two universal but contradictory ways of thinking about man's place in society, which coexist in some form (and probably must coexist) in every society.

Some thoughts on industrialization

I began this book by discussing some common assumptions about industrialization (pp. 1–3). These cannot be tested in a short study of a small sample. What follows is speculation and opinion supported by some evidence, a wider acquaintance with Indian industrial society, and reading.

One assumption was that industrial workers in countries like India are not 'committed' to industrial work and/or town life, and cannot adapt easily to bureaucratic organization. This assumption has its roots in functionalist modernization theory, and the idea of a folk – urban continuum, which sees the urban worker as someone uprooted from an integrated traditional society, where social groups

---

[9] See Dumont on the bhakti tradition (footnote 30, p. 85); also J. Parry, 'Egalitarian values in a hierarchical society', *South Asian Review* 7: 2 (1974), 95–121 (p. 95); Holmström, 'Religious change in an industrial city of South India', p. 28; and Ramanujan, *Speaking of Śiva*, 'Introduction'.

Some thoughts on industrialization

were in balance with each other and with their environment, and roles and expectations were clear. He becomes a 'marginal man' unable to adjust to a hostile environment, pulled back emotionally to the land, a prey to alienation and anomie.

With regard to urbanization, this view is no longer worth attacking: it is psychological guesswork, which exaggerates the impersonal horrors of the city and the pastoral contentment of country life, and underestimates human powers of creative adaptation. But the same kind of argument is applied to industrial organization, implying not only that one kind of hierarchical managerial structure – whether capitalist or state-controlled – is necessary for industrialization (which I doubt), but that workers must accept its legitimacy and identify with their roles in the production process; that they must see their future in this kind of structure; that they must have the right attitudes.[10]

This view is worth testing, but I think it is wrong, because it takes 'attitudes' as something relatively static, the result of 'socialization' or conditioning, modified by appropriate or inappropriate reactions to situations, rather than as creative *thought* in and about a situation.[11] Can workers' attitudes in this sense really be a critical factor making for successful industrialization? The Japanese may identify with their roles in the industrial system and feel loyal to their company, but this is not so in other advanced industrial countries, it was not when they were industrializing, and it is not in India now. Does it really make a critical difference to industrial performance whether workers are 'committed' to a firm or industrial life, or obedient, contented, militant or resentful?[12] The hypothesis about attitudes is not plausible

[10] The argument of Slotkin, Myers, Moore and Feldman (see footnote 2, p. 2).

[11] A behaviourist psychology tests and measures people's attitudes; dialectical sociology tries to understand and follow their thought. A good example of this sociology is J. H. Goldthorpe et al., The affluent worker in the class structure (Cambridge, 1969).

[12] See Morris, Emergence of an industrial labor force. This is a historical study, mainly of the Bombay cotton mills, also the Tata Iron and Steel Company at Jamshedpur. Morris argues that 'commitment' is really no problem; 'the creation of a disciplined labor force in a newly developing society is not particularly difficult' (p. 210). The 'indiscipline' and 'lack of commitment' employers complained of were the results of their own management practices and the workers' rational response to insecurity: 'the labor problems with which the industry had to contend did not flow primarily from the psychology of the work force or from the rigid traditions and structure of the rural social order. Such instability and indiscipline as did exist stemmed from the character of employer policies which were determined by the economic and technical characteristics of the enterprise and the competitive nature of the markets in which they operated' (p. 202).

143

Conclusions

if the observed behaviour can be explained more simply by the logic of the situation, as a rationally chosen course of action, when workers judge rightly that the main thing affecting careers is luck.

The second assumption was that commitment is no problem, but that in many countries it gives the best results in a paternalistic organization the worker can identify with, without sharply defined rights and duties: i.e. the Japanese model. Dore seems to suggest this in his *British factory – Japanese factory*, also that Britain and other western countries are 'catching up' with Japan in some ways (e.g. increasing job security and recognition of seniority in wage scales, gradual hierarchies without a sharp division between white-collar and manual workers).[13] Dore's book is a superb piece of comparative analysis, but I have doubts about the implied moral, which is (I think) that industrializing countries should embrace this form of organization consciously, because it is inevitable, and functionally best suited to a 'late-starting' economy: at least the expectation of lifetime employment in one firm is, if not the strong Japanese ethic of lifetime commitment. I find this too deterministic. Many forms of organization are probably compatible with industrialization, or with failure to industrialize; and the forms actually found in industrial countries probably depend as much on historical circumstances, ideologies and conscious choice as on the technical requirements of the industrial process.[14] The Japanese form of organization, with a lifetime commitment of the firm to the workers and vice versa, is not typical of modern industry in India, and it is hard to see any advantage in adopting it.

The third assumption was that industrial workers in countries like India are an 'aristocracy of labour' in a dual economy, either because this is inevitable in the early stages of industrialization, or because of wrong policies, e.g. too much capital-intensive large industry, or too much tenderness towards unions, or what Lipton calls 'urban bias' in planning.

I have tried to answer this question as far as it concerns these workers (once inside the organized sector citadel, they can expect to stay; they know they are fortunate; they are a middle class; the

[13] Dore (pp. 269–75) thinks 'paternalism' is the wrong word: he prefers 'welfare corporatism'.

[14] Dore asks – but does not try to answer – the question: 'How imperatively do the needs for handling complex technology and organization and for meeting demands for status equality impose identical institutional solutions on all advanced industrial economies, and how far do these "prerequisites" shape the character of industrial societies?' (p. 419).

Some thoughts on industrialization

wider benefits are spread quite widely among certain groups but not among the poorest). It raises further questions about the structure of the Indian and world economies, which are beyond the scope of this book. Are there really dual economies? If there are (e.g. in Latin America or Africa) is India one of them (since India is more self-sufficient than the typical dual economy, with a more diverse industrial economy and mor intermediate occupations and classes)? Is an 'aristocracy of labour' a class with a set part to play in a historical scenario, delaying the growth of working-class consciousness? Does import substitution give some Indian industries monopoly power, and if so how far can unions exploit this to their members' advantage? How do high wages abroad affect Indian wages, either by example or because of emigration? How far does a liberal welfare ideology of 'management' prevent private and public sector firms from maximizing profits?

The last assumption was that there are viable, and better, alternatives to high-technology industrialization, as distinct from complementary labour-intensive methods, or 'intermediate technologies'. This argument should be (but seldom is) distinguished from the argument for 'small-scale industries', meaning small *enterprises* which are often part of large industries and may have any level of technology. Indian small-scale industries receive considerable government help, including subsidies; and it is useful to contrast the respectable performance of some small-scale industries, which complement the organized sector, with the dismal failure, in economic and human terms, of many which are supposed to be alternatives to it.[15]

The debate is confused, because objectives are not clearly stated and conflicting objectives are not distinguished. The arguments for small enterprises with 'intermediate' or 'appropriate technology' are of four main kinds: that this is a better way to ensure all-round economic growth and distribution (doubtful, and certainly too simple);[16] that it makes for more equality and social justice in the process of industrialization, and less exploitation (very doubtful),[17]

---

[15] The best general discussion is Dhar and Lydall, *Role of small enterprises.* Lakshman, *Cottage and small-scale industries*, is a useful detailed account of small enterprises in the state – especially in the capital, Bangalore – their successes and problems, labour force, and interdependence with the organized sector.

[16] Deepak Lal argues convincingly (in 'Poverty and unemployment') that the costs of designing 'appropriate technologies' can also be very high, and that too much emphasis on technology and 'employment' diverts attention from the real problem, which is not employment but poverty. An appropriate *economic* policy would affect the choice of technology, often leading to adoption of more labour-intensive methods. And see J. N. Sinha, 'Poverty and unemployment' in Fonseca, ed., *Challenge of poverty in India*, pp. 159–65.

[17] See Dhar and Lydall, *Role of small enterprises*, pp. 24–7.

145

Conclusions

and that equality is either good in itself (I agree) or because it reduces social tensions (vague and possibly wrong); that a high standard of living and a 'consumer society' are false ideals and morally corrupting (roughly, the gandhian argument); and that small units and traditional technology upset the ecological balance less (which may be partly true, but would be more acceptable if it were not so obviously a case of the rich countries pulling up the industrial ladder after them).

These questions have obvious policy implications. Some are relatively neutral matters on which anyone can offer an opinion, but others raise political issues which put a foreign sociologist (especially one from a rich ex-colonial power) in a difficult moral position. It is not for me to give unasked-for advice, though my biases are obvious. 'Missionaries for development' may do more harm than good. Morally, it may even be healthier to justify 'development studies' in the West by enlightened self-interest: academic curiosity, improvement of theory, and our interest in keeping contact with countries like India. Of course this is not the whole story, but a saving fiction: if I were not involved with India and concerned about its problems, I would not have been drawn to this kind of work, and I hope Indians will find this research relevant to practical problems of development. But as a vantage-point from which to observe India, I prefer an academic ivory tower to a missionary pulpit.

To answer these questions we need many kinds of information: intensive anthropological studies of 'organized sector' workers and other groups directly or indirectly dependent on India's industrial economy, especially casual labourers and skilled men who make a career moving from one small workshop to another; local economic studies, e.g. on incomes and consumption patterns and the multiplier effects of industrial employment; demographic and migration studies; and an understanding both of large-scale economic and political trends and of rural and non-industrial India. This is an argument for more communication and debate between specialists working on related problems, especially in the same cities: not necessarily for large interdisciplinary research programmes, which can be over organized. 'Interdisciplinarity' is good practice but dangerous ideology.

The point is not to find the formula for development or a general theory of industrialization, for we shall never get either. It is to develop a more subtle and useful theory about the relation of thought and action to circumstances (super- and infrastructure, if you like)

146

than those implied in general theories of social change and 'modernization': to match people's experience of their world to other things we can know about that world. We have a wealth of surveys, questionnaires, and socio-economic studies, some of them very good: but the anthropology of urban work – in the sense of a careful description of workers' lives, which relates their action and thinking to their situation – has hardly begun in India.

BIBLIOGRAPHY

Bangalore Sub-Regional Labour Exchange. *Annual area employment market information report, period ending 31.3.1972* (duplicated). Bangalore, 1972.

Béteille, A. 'Ideas and interests: some conceptual problems in the study of social stratification in rural India', *International Social Science Journal*, 21:2 (1969), 219–35.

'Peasant associations and the agrarian class structure', *Contributions to Indian Sociology*, new series, 4 (1970), 126–39.

Beynon, H. and Blackburn, R. M. *Perceptions of work: variations within a factory.* Cambridge, 1972.

Bondurant, J. V. and Fisher, M. W. 'The concept of change in Hindu, socialist and neo-gandhian thought' in D. E. Smith (ed.), *South Asian politics and religion.* Princeton, 1966, pp. 235–48.

Census of India 1961. Paper 1 of 1963: 1961 Census – Religion. Delhi, 1967.

Census of India 1971. Paper 1 of 1971: Provisional population totals. Delhi, 1971.

Paper 1 of 1972: Final population. Delhi, 1972.

Series 14. Mysore, Part II–A: General population tables. Delhi, 1973.

Desai, I. P. *Some aspects of family in Mahuva: a sociological study of jointness in a small town.* Asia, Bombay, 1964.

De Souza, A. 'Education for employment' in A. J. Fonseca (ed.), *Challenge of poverty in India.* Vikas, Delhi, 1971, pp. 128–45.

Dhar, P. N. and Lydall, H. F. *The role of small enterprises in Indian economic development.* Asia, Bombay, 1961.

Dore, R. P. *City life in Japan: a study of a Tokyo ward.* London, 1958.

British factory – Japanese factory: the origins of national diversity in industrial relations. London, 1973.

Dumont, L. *Hierarchy and marriage alliance in South Indian kinship.* Occasional Papers of the Royal Anthropological Institute, 12. London, 1957.

'Marriage in India', *Contributions to Indian Sociology*, 7 (1964), 77–98.

Homo hierarchicus: the caste system and its implications. London, 1970.

'World renunciation in Indian religions', *Contributions to Indian Sociology*, 4 (1960), 33–62. Reprinted in Dumont, *Religion/politics and history in India.* Paris and The Hague, 1970.

Emmet, D. *Rules, roles and relations.* London, 1966.

Fonseca, A. J. (ed.). *Challenge of poverty in India.* Vikas, Delhi, 1971.

Frank, A. G. 'Sociology of development and underdevelopment of sociology', *Catalyst*, Summer 1967. Reprinted in Frank, *Latin America: underdevelopment or revolution.* New York, 1969, pp. 21–94.

Gellner, E. *Thought and change.* London, 1964.

Bibliography

Goldthorpe, J. H. *et al*. *The affluent worker: industrial attitudes and behaviour*. Cambridge, 1968.

The affluent worker in the class structure. Cambridge, 1969.

Government of Mysore. *Outline development plan for the Bangalore Metropolitan Region*. Bangalore, 1968.

Hart, H. C. 'Urban politics in Bombay: the meaning of community', *Economic Weekly*, special number, June 1960, 983–8.

Holmström, M. 'Action-sets and ideology: a municipal election in South India', *Contributions to Indian Sociology*, new series, 3 (1969), 76–93.

'Religious change in an industrial city of South India', *Journal of the Royal Asiatic Society* (1971), no. 1, 28–40.

'Caste and status in an Indian city', *Economic and Political Weekly*, 8 April 1972, 769–74.

Hoselitz, B. F. and Moore, W. E. (eds.). *Industrialization and society*. Paris, 1963.

Indian labour statistics 1972. (Published for the Labour Bureau, Simla.) Delhi, 1972.

Indian labour year book 1965. (Published for the Labour Bureau, Simla.) Delhi, 1967.

Indian labour year book 1968. (Published for the Labour Bureau, Simla.) Delhi, 1971.

Kapadia, K. M. and Devadas Pillai, S. *Industrialization and rural society*. Popular Prakashan, Bombay, 1972.

Lakshman, T. K. *Cottage and small-scale industries in Mysore*. Rao and Raghavan, Mysore City, 1966.

Lal, D. 'Poverty and unemployment: a question of policy', *South Asian Review* 5: 4 (1972), 305–12.

Lambert, R. D. *Workers, factories and social change in India*. Princeton, 1963.

Laslett, P. *The world we have lost*. London, 1965.

Lewis, Oscar. *The children of Sánchez*. Harmondsworth, 1964.

Lipton, M. 'Strategy for agriculture: urban bias and rural planning' in P. Streeten and M. Lipton (eds.), *The crisis of Indian planning*. London, 1968, pp. 83–147.

Lynch, O. *The politics of untouchability: social mobility and social change in a city of India*. New York, 1969.

Lyons, J. (ed.). *New horizons in linguistics*. Harmondsworth, 1970.

McClelland, D. C. 'The achievement motive in economic growth' in B. F. Hoselitz and W. E. Moore (eds.), *Industrialization and society*. Paris, 1963, pp. 74–96.

'The impulse to modernization' in M. Weiner (ed.), *Modernization*. New York, 1966, pp. 28–39.

Misra, B. B. *The Indian middle classes*. London, 1961.

Montejo, E. *The autobiography of a runaway slave*. Harmondsworth, 1970.

Moore, W. E. *Industrialization and labor*. Ithaca, 1951. Reprinted New York, 1965.

Moore, W. E. and Feldman, A. S. (eds.). *Labor commitment and social change in developing areas*. New York, 1960.

Bibliography

Morris, M. D. 'The labor market in India' in W. E. Moore and A. S. Feldman
    (eds.), *Labor commitment and social change in developing areas*. New York,
    1960, pp. 173–200.
*The emergence of an industrial labor force in India: a study of the Bombay cotton
    mills, 1854–1947*. Berkeley, 1965.
Myers, C. A. *Labor problems in the industrialization of India*. Cambridge, Mass.,
    1958.
Myrdal, G. *Asian drama: an inquiry into the poverty of nations*. London, 1968.
Niehoff, A. *Factory workers in India*. Milwaukee, 1959.
Parry, J. 'Egalitarian values in a hierarchical society', *South Asian Review*, 7:
    2 (1974), 95–121.
Parvathamma, C. *Politics and religion: a study of historical interaction between
    socio-political relationships in a Mysore village*. Stirling, New Delhi, 1971.
Pocock, D. F. 'The movement of castes', *Man*, 55 (May 1955), 71–2.
    '"Difference" in East Africa: a study of caste and religion in modern Indian
    society', *Southwestern Journal of Anthropology*, 13 : 4 (1957), 289–300.
    'Sociologies: urban and rural', *Contributions to Indian Sociology*, 4 (1960), 63–
    81. Reprinted in M. S. A. Rae (ed.), *Urban sociology in India*. New Delhi,
    1974, pp. 18–39.
    'The anthropology of time-reckoning', *Contributions to Indian Sociology*, 7
    (1964), 18–29.
    Kanbi and Patidar: a study of the Patidar community of Gujarat. Oxford, 1972.
Ramanujan, A. K. *Speaking of Siva*. Harmondsworth, 1973.
Rao, M. S. A. 'Occupational diversification and joint household organization',
    Contributions to Indian Sociology, new series, 2 (1968), 98–111.
Redfield, R. *The little community, and Peasant society and culture*. Chicago, 1960.
Report of the National Commission on Labour. (Ministry of Labour, Employ-
    ment and Rehabilitation.) Delhi, 1969.
Sharma, Ursula. *Rampal and his family*. London, 1971.
Sheth, N. R. *The social framework of an Indian factory*. Manchester, 1968.
Silverberg, J. (ed.). *Social mobility in the caste system in India*. The Hague, 1968.
Singer, M. *When a great tradition modernizes*. New York, 1972.
Singh, R. L. *Bangalore: an urban survey*. Varanasi, 1964.
Sinha, J. N. 'Poverty and unemployment' in A. J. Fonseca (ed.), *Challenge of
    poverty in India*, Vikas, Delhi, 1971, pp. 159–65.
Slotkin, J. S. *From field to factory*. New York, 1960.
Smith, D. E. (ed.). *South Asian politics and religion*. Princeton, 1966.
Srinivas, M. N. *Caste in modern India*. Asia, Bombay, 1962.
Streeten, P. and Lipton, M. (eds.). *The crisis of Indian planning*. London, 1968.
Turnham, D. *The employment problem in less developed countries*. Paris, 1971.
United Nations. *Mysore population study*. UN Population Series. Calcutta, 1961.
Weber, M. *The Protestant ethic and the spirit of capitalism*. London, 1930.
Weiner, M. (ed.). *Modernization: The dynamics of growth*. New York, 1966.
Wirth, L. 'Urbanism as a way of life', *American Journal of Sociology*, 44 : 1 (1938),
    1–24.

INDEX

'Aar·umugam', Harijan semi-skilled
  worker, president of union, case
  study, 92–3, 126
accident prevention and Workmen's
  Compensation, 61
admiration for conscientiousness, skill,
  learning and application, 60, 62–3
advertisements of job vacancies, 43;
  8 000 applications for 20 apprenticeships, 40; in English-language
  newspapers, 42
agarbathi (incense stick) makers, 16
age distribution of workers in sample
  factories, 20
All-India Trade Union Congress
  (AITUC), 66–8, 70, 96
allowances, see payments to workers
anthropology, see social anthropology
apprentices, 17, 40–1; Act of 1961, 40;
  obligatory quota in 'organized'
  sector, 9; percentages trained among
  workers in sample factories, 33
'aristocracy of labour' in a dual
  economy?, 144–5
attitudes and values (citing Hoselitz,
  McClelland, Moore, Myrdal etc.),
  3–4, 9–10, 142; see also
  industrialization; Japan, comparisons
  with; sociology of industrial India;
  urbanization
automatic machines, operators, 64
automobile parts, 17, 40
autoriksha drivers, 16

Baasava, founder or reformer of the
  Lingaayat sect, 119–20
backgrounds and living conditions
  of workers, 27–85
Bangalore city and District, 8–17; and
  Mysore State, population and sex
  ratio, 10–11; bus services, 75;

history of industries, 8–14; immigration from Madras (now Tamil Nadu)
  state, 9; industrial expansion in
  1971, 10; modern development,
  73–4; 'organized' and 'unorganized'
  sector employment statistics, 18–25;
  population, 9; population and
  employment statistics, 11–15, of
  males and females according to
  industrial categories, 13, 15
Béteille, A., quoted on significant
  distinctions and categories, 123
Bharatiya Mazdoor Sangh (BMS), trade
  union federation, 67
birthplaces of Bangalore workers,
  percentages from each of five
  Indian states and elsewhere, 26
blind workers, 61
bonuses, see payments to workers
Brahmans: alliance with Harijans
  under paternalistic management and
  in politics, 88; in managerial, skilled
  and most other jobs, 34; semi-
  skilled worker, communist union
  ex-official, brief case study, 97;
  skilled worker, case study, 101–2;
  steno-typists, case studies, 90–2,
  94–5
bribery, 49, 55
building and public works employment, 16

capitalism, welfare type, prevailing
  form in India, 125
car components, see automobile parts
careers: analytically significant
  distinctions and categories, 53,
  122–3; as distinguished from 'jobs',
  138–9; as stage or incident in an
  idealistically motivated lifetime,
  116–17, 133; assumed here to

mean movement up the ladder of income, with its concomitants, 52; attempted analysis from workers' point of view, 122–35; beginning when once inside the 'citadel', 52; employment as stage or incident before a career, three case studies, 114–16, 132–3; factory hierarchy closer to British than Japanese, 53, 62; grading of jobs according to degree of skill, 53; judgments of fact and value, 125; normally annual steps and increments within each grade, 52; percentages of permanent, temporary etc. in one private factory, 59; politics or unions as alternatives to factory careers, 98–100, 128; three methodological steps in analysing, 123–4; *see also* promotion

case studies, 86–8; methodology, 86–8, 135

caste: and intermarriage, analysis of opinions, 79, 83; bhakti or devotional religion allowing free choice of personal life, 84–5; comparison (not identification) with factory hierarchy, 53; hierarchy and 'sub-castes', different kinds of significance, traditional ideology, effects on marriage and social mobility, 32–4; in case studies, 89–95 *passim*; of workers' fathers and grandfathers, 34–5; old 'pollution' rules, 81; relation to language groups, 30; Tigal·as farming caste, 36n, *see also* Lingaayat sect; religion

casual workers, 16

Centre for Indian Trade Unions (CITU), 66

changing jobs by moving to another factory, 57; loss of retirement gratuity, 57

child labour, in 'unorganized sector', 13

childhood environment: birthplaces of Bangalore workers, 26; occupations and castes or religions of workers' fathers and grandfathers, 34–5, of present workers, 200

'chit funds' (rotating credit associations), 56, 78

Christians, percentages in sample factories and in Bangalore population, 25; better educated, well placed to find factory work, 31; immigrants from Kerala (ancient Syrian church), 32, 34; marriage with Hindus, 30

'citadel' of permanent employment, the one big prize, 41, 46; identified with security and relative prosperity, 137; *see also* careers; 'job' and 'career'

class distinctions: Indian usage of 'middle class' and 'working class', 137–8; relevance, 123

clerical skills, percentages of certificate holders in, 24

clubs and associations, religious, factory or factory-township based, 72–3; management support, 73

commitment, to a firm, to industrial life, 2–3, 62, 137, 143–4; *see also* Japan, comparisons with

'communalism', excessive attachment to own 'community', 30, 36–7

Communist Party of India (CPI), 66–7

Communist Party of India (Marxist) (CPI (M) or CPM), 66, 95–6

'communities', relation to language groups, 30

Congress Party, 66; its kind of socialism, 70

contented workers, case studies of two, 105–6

contraceptives, 84, 95, 102

corruption, 111

cost of living index ('Simla scale'), 58

Cottage and small-scale industries in Mysore, by T. K. Lakshman, quoted, 16–17

country life, no nostalgia for by landless labourers, 29

craftsmanship training, among workers in sample factories, 24

'cultural' associations, 73

Dearness Allowance, negotiated through unions, effect on differentials, 21, 58–9

Index

de Souza, A., cited on apprenticeship schemes and ITIs, 41
'Dhanaraaj', Harijan, group leader, case study, 156–7
disabled employees, 61
disciplinary action, 64, 71
dismissal, made difficult for managements, 55
'divine right of the middle class', 50, 69, 102
DMK (Dravida Munnetra Kazhagam), Tamil-populist party, 73
draftsman's work, 63, 65

earnings, *see* payments to workers
education, training and qualifications, 38–42; age proportions of workers holding SSLC or technical qualifications, 39; importance of paper qualifications, 41; Intermediate or Pre-University examinations, 40; school conditions not good, 39–40; technical training for apprentices, 40; training abroad, 41, 57; women's situation different, 39, *and see* women workers; *see also* engineering
educational level, analysis for sample factories, 23
'efficiency', 60
Employees' State Insurance (ESI), 52, 59–61; clinics, 61
engineering, diplomas and licentiates, 41; equivalent experience of skilled work?, 41; percentages of holders in sample factories, 24
English language speakers, 25
experience, falsely claimed, 51

Factories Act, 17–18; widely evaded in small workshops, 12–13
factory buses, 75
factory football teams, practice in working hours, 73
factory owner's kith and kin, three case studies, 106–8, 130
factory townships, 74
factory workers: 'a distinctive Indian industrial culture', 27; who they are, whether a privileged élite, how they see their situation, 136–7

family planning, 84, 94–5, 102
'fine arts clubs', 73
'folk–urban continuum', shorter than 'urbanization' theory suggests, 29–30
foundries, *see* 'machine-shop-cum-foundries

Gandhian moral repudiation of high standard of living, 146
'Gangaadharan', Harijan, skilled worker in a public sector factory, case study, 113
'Goovindappa' and 'Venkat araaman' contented workers, case studies, 105–6
grievances, 'individual' and 'group', 56, 67, 71

hard or hopeless cases, 102–5, 129
Harijans (Scheduled Caste Hindus, formerly 'Untouchables'): Aadi Draavid as (modern name for Tamil-speaking Harijans), immigrants less bound to traditional low-grade work than those speaking Kannad a or Telugu, 32, 34; alliance with Brahmans under paternalistic management and in politics, 88; as cleaners and watchmen, in skilled and semi-skilled jobs, 34; case studies, 92, 112–13; educational concessions and job reservation (aiding upward mobility, formerly owed sometimes to army or police background), 34; employment quota, 48; obligatory quota in public sector, lower average pay, 33; percentages in sample factories, 25; righting of former injustice to, 49, 92; skilled workers who are union officials, case studies, 93–4
Hind Mazdoor Sabha (HMS), breakaway socialist trade union federation, 66–7
Hindi or Urdu language speakers, 25
Hinduism, 85; ethics compared with those of Lingaayat ideology, 120–1; fatalism contrasted with American

progressive mentality, 108–9;
little self-conscious religious community feeling, 31; middle caste in most jobs except cleaning, 34; new ideal of social service, 117; paternalistic management, 88, 126; percentages (other than Harijans) in sample factories and in Bangalore population, 25; *see also* caste; Harijans; Lingaayat
Hindustan Aircraft factory, 9
holidays, annual and casual leave, 61
home life, 73–9
household size, 76–7
housing, 74–5
Hubli-Dharwar (town), population, 11

idealistic, reforming, middle-class workers, 100–2, 128–9
ideologies: loyalty to, 88; of militant unionists dedicated to interests of the 'working class', 95–8, 127–8; of moderate social reform and service to the nation, 100–2, 128–9; of personal achievement-oriented ambition, case studies, 108–10, 131; politico-religious, 111; relation to actions, 91–2; *see also* 'communalism'; Lingaayat
immigrants, 34–5; of rural origin, 28–9
incomes, *see* payment to workers
Indian Institute of Science, 9
Indian labour statistics 1972, 12
Indian National Trade Union Congress (INTUC), 66, 96
individual differences of attitude to employment, 9–10
Industrial Training Institutes (ITI), 9, 38, 40–1; percentages of workers in sample factories trained at, 24; trainees recruited by factories directly from, 43
industrialization, 142–3; authors quoted or cited on (Feldman, Moore, Slotkin etc.), 1–3, 148–50; doubtful ideological assumptions, 2–4; should not be identified with urbanization, 1–2; workers' attitudes towards, 2–4; *see also* commit-

ment; small-scale industries innovations, rewards to workers suggesting, 56, 60
'intermediate technologies', *see* small-scale industries

Jan Sangh, semi-religious right-wing nationalist party, 67, 70, 89, 94, 102
'Janardan', skilled worker, union official, case study, 93–4
Japan, comparisons with, 8; Dore, R., *British factory – Japanese factory*, quoted, 53, 57, 62; 'moral community' of human not merely functional relations, 64
Japanese ethic of 'lifetime commitment', 144
'job' and 'career': in contrasted senses, 4, 124, 140; relation of 'job' to 'career', 138–9
job finding: by advertised job vacancies, 28; by bribery and by unfair influence, 49; helped by relatives or influential outsiders, 43, 49; letters and forms of application, 44; luck in getting jobs or promotion, 41, 46, 50; *see also* recruitment and promotion
'jobs': ambiguity of term (Emmet cited), 124; 'jobs' incidental to starting a 'career', 181–2, 114–16, 132
joint families and households, 76–8

Kannada communalist parties and cultural organizations, 36–7
Kannada language speakers, (Kannadigas); 25, 30, 34; gaining on Tamil in Bangalore, 36; Kannadigas' antipathy to Tamil and Malayali immigrants, 37–8, 165; preference in recruitment, 47
Karnataka (formerly Mysore State), 8
'Kempayya', semi-skilled worker in a public sector factory, case study, 29, 114–15
Kerala, immigrants from, 28; Syrian Christians and other immigrants from Kerala (ancient Syrian church), 32, 34
'Krisnamuurti', Brahman in a super-

visory job, case study, 113–14
'Kumaar', Harijan chargehand with
politico-religious indeology, case
study, 111–12

Lakshman, T.K., quoted, 16–17
land reform: by voluntary sacrifice or
by compulsion?, 102
language consciousness: cutting across
caste boundaries, 32; Kannadigas'
antipathy to Tamil speakers, 111,
157; partly a code for class
consciousness, also a claim to
solidarity across caste lines, 37–8
languages, percentages speaking
Kannada, Tamil, Telugu, Hindi or
Urdu etc., in sample factories and
Bangalore, 25
'leadership', as end in itself, 139
length of service, median in sample
factories, 21
Life Insurance Corporation (govern-
mental), 62
'lifetime commitment', *see* commitment
Lingaayat (or Viirashaiva) sect,
motivated by a variant of the
'Protestant ethic', 118–21, 134
'Lingaraaj', draftsman, of Lingaayat
Weaver caste, case study, 119–20
literacy rate comparisons, 11

'machine-shop-cum-foundries', 17
management files of workers'
particulars, 19–20
market porters, 16
marriage, 117–22; and caste (citing
Dumont), 54, 101, 113; and size of
households, 36; for love, 82–3,
former caste endogamy weakening,
81–2; hypergamy, 53; intercaste, 80,
90, 93–5, 113, 116, and inter-
community, 31–2, old rules becoming
irrelevant, 80; of Harijans with other
castes, 113
maternity leave, 93
'merit', 49–50; *see also* promotion
methodology, 1–10, 86–8; case studies,
86–8, of 104 workers from four
factories, 6–8; doubtful ideological

assumptions, 2–4; judgments of fact
and value, 125; kinds of evidence,
6–8; three questions: place of
factory workers in Indian society,
their own understanding of their
situation, ideas of 'job' and 'career',
5–6; unstratified systematic random
sampling of four factories' management files, 18–26; *see also* careers
'Michael', Christian toolmaker from
Kerala, case study, 108–9
middle-aged workers ambitious for proper careers when qualified for
retirement benefit, 116
'middle' and 'working classes', 50; terms
used interchangeably, 71, 95; *see
also* class distinctions
migration: different patterns in
North and South India, 11; sometimes difficult, seldom traumatic,
28
money-lending and borrowing, 78
'moonlighting', multiple employment,
56
Mudaliaars from Tamil Nadu, 32, 34
Muslims: percentages in sample
factories and in Bangalore, 25; some
in better-paid skilled jobs, 31
Mysore State (now Karnataka), 8

'Naagaraajan', Brahman steno-typist,
case study, 90–2
Naidu caste, 30
Naidus from Andhra, 32, 34
'Narasappa', 'Raajendra', 'Kumaarasvaami', three case studies of
factory owner's kith and kin, 106–8,
130
'Nataraajan', Brahman toolmaker,
pursuing a religious ideal of non-
attachment, case study, 117
National Commission on Labour,
Report cited, 51
nationalization, demanded by communists, 68–9

office jobs, 19
Okkaligas from Mysore, 32, 34
'organized' and 'unorganized' sectors,
9–12, 14; accident prevention, 61;

Index

industrial workers as percentage of
all workers and of total population
in India's six largest cities, 14;
'unorganized sector', no proper
statistics available, 15; unorganized
small non-industrial establishments,
enterprises and individual workers,
14–18; *see also under* Bangalore;
Factories Act; small workshops
origins of workers, urban and rural, 28

paper qualifications, increased
importance, 56
'paternalism', 70
pavement vendors' union, 96
payments to workers, 58–9; basic pay
comparisons, no reflection of
total earnings, 20–1; basic salaries,
four sample factories, 21; 'efficiency'
bonus in one private factory, 60;
higher in private than public sector,
21; incentive bonuses, overtime,
house rent allowances, fringe
benefits, 58; median basic pay in
four factories, 58; no unemployment pay, 61; private factory
workers' grades of skill, salaries,
conditions of employment, tabular
analyses 59; *see also* Dearness
Allowance; Harijans
permanent employment, *see* 'citadel'
personnel officers, 69; conversations on
recruitment policies, 46–8
pleasure in work, 60, 62–4
Pocock, D. F., cited, 29–30
political parties: Kannada communalists, 36; *see also* Communist Party
of India; Congress Party; DMK;
Jan Sangh; Republican Party
polytechnics, 8, 40–1
population, 9
'Prabhaakar', skilled worker in a
private factory, case study, 114–15
production consciousness, 60
promotion, 41; analysis showing
average once in every 5.66 years'
service, 54; by seniority rather than
'merit', 54–6; management prerogative, but subject to union

pressure, 55; merit and luck, 50;
sometimes through reclassification of
a whole group of workers, 54
Provident Fund, 59, 78
public sector, over-recruitment to
reduce unemployment, 111
public and private sectors, 9–10;
compared, 98–9, as regards security
and opportunity, 110

'Raajaraam', skilled worker, about 35,
thinks only of retirement, case study,
116
'Raamakrisn a, 'Deevaraaj', 'Muniappa',
'Paapann a', 'Raaju', 'Tyaagaraajan',
workers with no alternative openings, brief case studies, 10
'Raamayya', semi-skilled worker with
no alternative openings, case study,
103
Ramanujan, A. K., translator of
Lingaayat lyrics, 120–1
recruitment and promotion: by
contacts + 'merit' in private
sector, 44; fluctuations, 46; for
public sector, more formal, bureaucratic and 'fairer', giving more
weight to paper qualifications, 49;
ITI diploma useful, not essential
for semi-skilled jobs, 48; largely a
matter of luck, 139; number of
previous jobs and age at appointment to present job, 45; percentages
recruited by various methods, 43;
policies, and criteria for appointment, 46–9; preference to
employees' relatives, 48; *see also*
job finding
religion: as indicator of background,
culture and community, 31; case
study sample analysis covering 77
Hindus by caste, 21 Christians by
denomination, 5 Muslims, 1 Jain, 32;
neo-Buddhism of Dr B.R. Ambedkar,
118; of workers' fathers and
grandfathers, 34–5; relation to
language groups, 30; the most clear-
cut 'community', 30; *see also*
Christians; Hinduism, Muslims, 30

156

remittances to rural relatives, 77–8
repetitive, dull, hard, hot or
    exhausting work, 62–3
Republican Party (all-Harijan), 97
'Rudrappa', machine operator of the
    Lingaayat sect, case study, 119–20
rural to urban migration, 28–9

salaries, *see* payments to workers
sample factories, statistics for two in
    public and two in private sector,
    18–19
schools, *see* education, training and
    qualifications
security versus opportunity, 110–14,
    130, 139
Senior School Leaving Certificate
    (SSLC), 38–41; eligibility of holders
    (and even of 'SSLC Failed') for
    Industrial Training Institutes, 38;
    held by majority in sample factories,
    22; increasingly required for any
    factory work, 38–9
sex ratio comparisons, 11
sick leave, ESI clinics, 61
Sinha, J. N., quoted on unemployment,
    51
skilled workers, in small engineering
    workshops, 17–18
Small Industries Service Institutes, 18n
small workshops (engineering etc.), 9,
    16–18; severe problems, marginal
    existence, low wages, no security or
    social benefits, 17–18
small-scale industries receiving
    government help, 145–6
social anthropology: 'industrial society'
    may be compatible with many
    ideologies, 140; man in society,
    alternative models, 140–2; pioneer-
    ing studies cited, 8; urban not
    divisible from rural, 29; *see also*
    class distinctions
Social Welfare Societies, 61
sociology of industrial India,
    problems in, 1–3; evolutionary
    models, unilinear and other (Gellner
    cited), 2; 'folk–urban continuum'
    assumption, 29–30

'Sriinivaas', Brahman steno-typist, case
    study, 94–5
Srinivas, M. N., cited, 6
street vendors, 16
strikes, 66, 71, 93
'Subramaniam', middle-caste Tamil,
    case study, 110–11
'Sundaram', skilled Brahman worker,
    case study, 101–2
supervisors, foremen, chargehands and
    group leaders, 64
Swami Vivekananda, *see* Vivekananda
syntagmatic and paradigmatic relation-
    ships, 124–5

Tamil language speakers, 25, 30
Tamil Nadu, immigrants from North
    Arcot District, 28
Tamil-populist DMK 'social work'
    groups, 73
technical qualifications: analysis of
    holders in sample factories, 24;
    certificates or diplomas, 10
Telugu language speakers, 25, 30, 34
textile mills, 8, 18
'Thomas', Catholic skilled worker,
    communist union official, case study,
    96–7
time-and-motion study, 116
town and country life, comparison, 29;
    see also urban and rural; 'folk–urban
    continuum'
trade unions, 55–5, 65–72; accepted
    by almost all, usually subsidized by
    managements, 67; agreements
    regulating promotion, 55; Centre for
    Indian Trade Unions (CITU), break-
    away from AITUC to support
    CPI(M), 66; 'citadel' mentality of
    some members, 72; 'ideological',
    'pragmatic' and 'transactional' styles,
    68–71; in public sector factories,
    leaders and committee members,
    71–2; leadership careers, 98–100,
    128; local arrangements, informal
    negotiations, formal meetings,
    ideologies, operational styles, social
    and sporting activities, 68–71;
    national federations linked with

political parties, 66–7, 96, *and see under individual parties*; officials, not paid, 67; one factory, one union–no craft unions, 65; *see also* strikes

unemployment, 51, 61; no unemployment pay, 61
unions, *see* trade unions
university-qualified workers in sample factories, 23
urban and rural, not distinct, 29–30
urbanization, 143; authors cited on (Lal, Lipton, Redfield, Wirth), 2–3, 148–50; not identical with industrialization, 2–3; *see also under* Bangalore city and District

vasectomy, 84
Vivekananda, Swami, 89–91, 102

wages, *see* payments to workers
women workers, 13, 19, 22–3, 65; education and training, 65; night shifts forbidden, 61; percentage in four sample factories, 19; *see also* sex ratio comparisons
worker participation in factory affairs, 73
workers' attitudes, 143; feeling of being different (from peasants etc.), 27
'working class' and 'middle class', terms used interchangeably, 71, 95; *see also* class distinctions
working hours and conditions, 61–4
Workmen's Compensation, 61

Yaadava, Naidu 'subcaste' or Goll·a caste, 30

For EU product safety concerns, contact us at Calle de José Abascal, 56–1°, 28003 Madrid, Spain or eugpsr@cambridge.org.

www.ingramcontent.com/pod-product-compliance
Ingram Content Group UK Ltd.
Pitfield, Milton Keynes, MK11 3LW, UK
UKHW012341130625
459647UK00009B/447